Similar Hearts

Africa

Reflections and True Stories About Life, Love, Faith, and Hidden Treasure

TIMOTHY LEHMAN

AuthorHouse™
1663 Liberty Drive
Bloomington, IN 47403
www.authorhouse.com
Phone: 833-262-8899

Because of the dynamic nature of the Internet, any web addresses or links contained in this book may have changed since publication and may no longer be valid. The views expressed in this work are solely those of the author and do not necessarily reflect the views of the publisher, and the publisher hereby disclaims any responsibility for them.

Any people depicted in stock imagery provided by Getty Images are models, and such images are being used for illustrative purposes only. Certain stock imagery © Getty Images.

This book is printed on acid-free paper.

Unless otherwise identified, "Scripture quotations taken from the New American Standard Bible® (NASB), Copyright © 1960, 1962, 1963, 1968, 1971, 1972, 1973, 1975, 1977, 1995 by The Lockman Foundation Used by permission. HYPERLINK "http://www.Lockman.org"

Scripture taken from the HOLY BIBLE, NEW INTERNATIONAL VERSION®. NIV®. Copyright © 1973, 1978, 1984 by International Bible Society. Used by permission of Zondervan. All rights reserved worldwide.

Cover and chapter illustrations 1,3,7,16,17,22,24, and Africa Map by Magdolna Madai, Orosháza, Hungary. Chapter illustrations 2,11,12, and 19 by Dominika Darabos, Szentes, Hungary.

ISBN: 978-1-6655-4620-1 (sc)
ISBN: 978-1-6655-4621-8 (e)

Print information available on the last page.

Published by AuthorHouse 12/09/2021

authorHOUSE®

SIMILAR HEARTS
AFRICA

Reflections and true stories about life,
love, faith, and hidden treasure…

-By Timothy Lehman

Dedication

I dedicate this book to our Heavenly Father, King Jesus/Yeshua, and the Holy Spirit: for designing and creating me and for granting me the gifts of life and of eternal life; for giving me a loving family and community of faith to grow up in; for giving me the opportunity to gain an education; for protecting me through my turbulent teenage years; for helping me discover meaningful, enjoyable work where I could learn to love, serve, and bless others; for teaching me through so many different people and situations what it means to walk faithfully with God; for correcting me and restoring me when I have gotten off of the path of obedience and turned away; for continuing to love and guide me through the many ups and down of the past years; for teaching me through my students here in Hungary how to open my heart and trust Him and others once again; for bringing me to Jerusalem six times to visit the City of the Great King and to participate in The Convocation of the House of Prayer For All Nations four times; for creating a miracle in my heart there in Jerusalem; for providing the inspiration through someone He introduced to me there to write this book; for giving me the privilege of continuing the conversation with that someone over the last three months of 2018; for promising to give me a good future and a hope, and for continuously calling me to follow Him in the adventure of new life to which He has called each of us.

I give thanks to God for all of those who have touched, influenced, and blessed my life and faith journey, but I especially thank Him for my mother, Elsie Lehman, who, throughout her daily life and walk with the Lord, showed me consistently what it means to love and to serve with joy, honor, great faith, creativity, resourcefulness, and perseverance. Almost everything important in life that I have needed to know, I learned from my mother. I desire to follow her example and be a faithful steward of all that has been entrusted to me.

Finally, I give thanks for my wonderful, amazing Aunt Alice Schellenberg, who, after many years of serving God in Kenya with my Uncle John Schellenberg, went home to be with the Lord at the age of 105. Aunt Alice was a dedicated, faithful prayer warrior, who interceded daily for each of our extended family.

Acknowledgments

I would like to thank Pastor Tom Hess, the founder of The Jerusalem House of Prayer for All Nations, and his wife, Pastor Kate Hess, for their unswerving dedication to obeying the call of God upon their lives, and for their passion and commitment to seeing the Kingdom of God established here on earth.

Also, I would like to say thank you to Christine and Sodapop Ch. Jeanville, Founders and Directors of Machol Danser la Vie, for sharing vital teachings about how beautifully expressive dance and movement are meant to be in the life and worship of every believer. I am also grateful to Christine and Sodapop for living out a wonderful, powerful model of what marriage and ministry partnership look like in real life.

In addition, I would like to recognize and thank Alíz Schiller and Anna Magyari, for their constant prayer agreement support in every situation and need.

I would like to thank my amazing siblings: Harold, David, Peter, Mary, James, and Cynthia and their spouses and families, for all of their love and support, especially my sister Cynthia, who has helped me with so many practical arrangements and details over the years.

In addition, I would like to thank those individuals and families who have opened their hearts and homes to me on many occasions and given me a place to sojourn during those periods when I was traveling back and forth between Hungary and the United States. Thank you to Phyllis and John Sauder, Al and Diane Honer, Judy Honer and Mundy Hepburn, Bill and Sharyn Nelson, Price and Peggy van der Swaagh, and Carl and Ruth Muller, for your many kindnesses and warm hospitality.

Also, I would like to thank Erzsébet Aranyi and Father Ödön Nemes, for sharing a powerful word from the Lord with me in 2003 which literally helped save my life when I was struggling to keep my head above water. Three years ago, Erzsébet and her husband, Sándor, helped me through another challenging period, and I thank both of them for their prayers and support.

For their prayer support and encouragement, I would like to thank the members and families of the Szentes Baptist Congregation, especially Sándor Török and Sándor Kis-Hajdú.

For the brilliant, inspiring illustrations which they have created for this book, I would like to recognize and thank Magdolna Madai, Orosháza, and Dominika Darabos, Szentes.

For his invaluable technical assistance in preparing the manuscript, I would like to thank Zoltán Mucsi.

For her careful reading through of the manuscript and providing essential content and editing feedback, I would like to say a special thank you to my friend, Petra Nádor.

For his deep sensitivity to the Holy Spirit and for sharing a word of knowledge with me about similar hearts, which opened the door to the events that led to the writing of this book, I would like to thank my wonderful brother in the Lord, Marek, from the Czech Republic.

Finally, I would like to thank Annamária, from Slovakia: a dear friend and sister in the Lord, for the gifts of her friendship, understanding, and prayer support, and for the conversations she shared with me about life, love, faith, and the road ahead. This book would never have been written without her, and I am grateful to God and to her for her inspirational example of pioneering faith and trust in God, His goodness, mercy, and provision.

The kingdom of heaven

is like a treasure

hidden in the field;

which a man found and hid;

and from joy over it

he goes and sells all that he has,

and buys that field.

(Matthew 13:44)

Contents

Foreword

It is with the greatest pleasure that I have come to know Timothy Lehman as my true brother in the Lord. I have found in his book the same heart's cry, which is to find that one person whom God has for each of us. Reading these chapters and the testimonies shared within has caused me to hunger more for God's hand in my future marriage, every step all the way, withholding nothing from Him. God is love, and He alone can fill us, so that we may be able to fully and selflessly love others. One cannot help but sense the intense desire for love and the longing for a life partner that echo through these pages, as the author shares his own personal journey. The writer knows full well just how challenging it can be to find that one person with whom one can build a meaningful and lasting relationship capable of successfully navigating the unique challenges of our present era.

I believe that many people also share in their hearts this overwhelming desire to experience true love, as evidenced by the many dating agencies and relationship chat shows in existence today. It would seem as if nearly everyone is looking for someone, and the more dating sites and match-making programs available, the more confused, frustrated, and discouraged people become–nevertheless, the search continues. If you have been wondering how you will ever meet that special person and have been reluctant to trust again, or perhaps you have lost hope and confidence in marriage itself, I encourage you to not despair, but instead to read through what follows from cover to cover. *Similar Hearts* was written with all of us in mind, regardless of age, financial status, or cultural background. It is the book of the moment, and it speaks to all people.

Love is indeed the only answer to the questions of our modern-day world, especially to matters of the heart. I am persuaded that the reader will be stirred here to search the depths and heights of the kind of love that alone can unite two people to create something phenomenal and magical. As you immerse yourself in the pages of this book, may you also invite God to deposit something fresh into your heart, so that you may also become that special person someone is searching and praying for.

As you read *Similar Hearts*, may the Lord also order and direct your steps into a life of unspeakable joy, coupled with unquenchable love. God is a matchmaker, and He is inviting you to partner with Him, so that He can make your relationships blossom, enriched with the unconditional love of God. In Song of Solomon 8: 6-7 we find: *"For love is as strong as death...Many waters cannot quench love."* (NASB)

This describes the conquest of love— nothing can surpass its power. You will find that this book will open your eyes to the simplicity yet unparalleled strength of love. The author explores the many aspects of love, for instance, the capacity of love, the commitment of love, the communion of love, the cost of love, as well as the rewards of love.

Similar Hearts has been written so that we may revive our hopes and expectations of finding that special person designed just for us. Whatever our definitions or perceptions of love are, God desires to take us into the deeper layers of love which He has placed within us. Let us open our eyes to the resilience and endless possibilities of love. This book is filled with practical things we can engage in as we prepare to meet that unique, one-in-a-million person whose heart is similar to ours.

Allow yourself to step fully into the pages of this book. It is time to forget the fear of rejection and embrace the compelling message of *Similar Hearts*. May you be blessed beyond measure as you continue the journey of discovering your hidden treasure.

Julita Nyagura

Introduction

People used to believe that man couldn't fly. Then, one day, a few inventors with inquisitive minds started dreaming about the possibility of constructing something that would carry them up into the air and allow them to glide along on air currents. They imagined it, developed a prototype, and tested it, but it didn't work. They went back to the drawing board, made some modifications, and tried it again—again—and again. Finally, the day came when their model at last lifted off the ground and rose into the air.

Ages ago, the Lord God dreamed about, created, then fashioned the first man and woman, Adam and Eve, to His perfect specifications. He breathed the breath of His Spirit into them, gave them free will, and placed them in the Garden of Eden: a place of indescribable beauty, peace, joy, and delight. He desired to have a family of beloved sons and daughters who would be like Him—endowed with the ability to create, be fruitful, and exercise wise, responsible stewardship over their area of dominion, the earth.

God also imagined and established the perfect prototype for marriage: a beautiful, glorious, and intimate partnership between Adam and Eve. He gave them similar hearts, and they only had eyes for each other. The design was perfect. The prototype lifted off the ground during the first test flight, and then it soared! It was Heaven on earth, just as the Lord God had intended. The Lord God gave them specific instructions, and He visited them in the garden every evening. Then, Eve and Adam disregarded one of the commands they had been given and listened to the wrong voice, which resulted in their losing everything God had wonderfully and graciously provided them.

This book is about God's heart to restore us to fullness of relationship and intimacy with Himself and one another, and to restore marriage. He designed marriage for us so we could experience all of the delight, joy, adventure, and ecstasy possible when a man and woman surrender their lives and hearts to Him and invite Him to be at the very center of their relationship. God doesn't want any couple to step into marriage with anything less than a full understanding of the huge potential for their holy union to become a shining star that will reflect His goodness, glory, and presence. The Lord desires to supernaturally touch and transform each couple's areas of influence to such an extent, that what is seen and felt there will begin to look like the Garden of Eden once again.

I believe God is saying to us, *"I want you to see what I see; dream what I dream; create what I can help you create. I desire to restore everything that has been lost, if you'll let Me."*

Jesus said, *"The things impossible with men are possible with God."* (Luke 18:27 NASB)

Do you dare to believe that? Do you want that? Are you willing to look beyond the veil of the limited confines of our human experiences in marriage and invite the Designer and Creator of the universe to do the impossible in your relationship? Will you step out in faith, take the leap, go where few men and women have ever gone before, and reach for the sky? Will you allow God Himself to help you create His type of marriage in you and your beloved? This is not a theoretical question; this is God's special invitation to you, and it's the chance of a lifetime!

Whether you are single, romantically challenged, married, separated, divorced, widowed or other, if your answer is yes, this book is for you. I should caution you, however: if you decide to embark on this amazing journey, it may cost you everything, but the reward will be *everything* He has promised!

Chapter 1: In the Beginning

The Lord God formed the man from the dust from the ground and breathed into his nostrils the breath of life, and the man became a living being. Now the Lord God had planted a garden in the east, in Eden; and there He put the man He had formed. And the Lord God made all kinds of trees grow out of the ground—trees that were pleasing to the eye and good for food. In the middle of the garden were the tree of life and the tree of the knowledge of good and evil. (Genesis 2:7–9 NIV)

Then the Lord God took the man and put him into the Garden of Eden to work it and take care of it. And the Lord God commanded the man, "You are free to eat from any tree in the garden; but you must not eat from the tree of the knowledge of good and evil, for when you eat from it you shall surely die."

The Lord God said, "It is not good for the man to be alone. I will make him a helper suitable for him." Now the Lord God had formed out of the ground all the beasts of the field and all the birds of the air. He brought them to the man to see what he would name them; and whatever the man called each living creature, that was its name. So the man gave names to all the livestock, the birds of the air and to all the beasts of the field. But for Adam no suitable helper was found. (Genesis 2:15–20 NIV)

So the Lord God caused a deep sleep to fall upon the man, and he slept; then He took one of his ribs, and closed up the flesh at that place. And the Lord God fashioned into a woman the rib which He had taken from the man, and brought her to the man. And the man said, "This is now bone of my bones, and flesh of my flesh; She shall be called Woman, because she was taken out of Man."

For this reason a man shall leave his father and his mother, and shall cleave to his wife; and they shall become one flesh. And the man and his wife were both naked and were not ashamed. (Genesis 2:21–25 NASB)

Have you ever wondered what it must have been like there, in the Garden of Eden, at the very beginning? Can you picture a paradise with two perfect people, Adam and Eve, who were given free will, walked with God in the garden, enjoyed His presence, and conversed with Him daily? Can you imagine heartfelt, intimate communication and relationship among a man, a woman, and God—the Designer and Creator of all things?

Have you imagined what Adam's first conversation with Eve was like? I mean, what would you say if you were Adam, and the Lord suddenly presented you with this stunningly beautiful creature who took your breath away, made your heart beat a million times a minute, and filled you with such joy and delight that you struggled to find words to express all of that?

When the Lord brought Eve to Adam, Adam responded by saying, *"This is now bone of my bones, and flesh of my flesh; she shall be called Woman, because she was taken out of Man"* (Genesis 2:23–25 NASB). Those were the words which Adam used to say yes to the person the Lord had fashioned and then presented to him. God desired that Adam would no longer be alone, that he would have an equal partner to share all of life with—someone with whom to carry out the responsibilities God had entrusted to him, and, subsequently, to the two of them.

Yet, what did Adam say to Eve after that and Eve to him? What did they talk about during that first human exchange of words? How long did that last? What did they feel and experience in that first perfect conversation, in that immaculate world, in that beautiful garden filled with the presence, love, joy, and peace of the Lord? I'm deeply curious about that! None of us really knows; we can speculate, but that's about it. It is a complete mystery—yet, a lovely one to contemplate.

Have you ever had a totally open, free, beautiful, honest, and joyful conversation with someone—a delightfully spontaneous, vivacious, and attractive person of the opposite sex? Have you engaged in a conversation that just flowed with such ease and comfort that you felt, as if on some level, you had known that person all your life, even though you just met? Have you ever experienced such a profoundly touching heart connection with another person, within the space of a few short hours, that you sensed your whole life would never be the same from that moment onward?

There's only been one time in my life when I've experienced this. It was in mid-September 2018, over dinner with someone at a Christian convocation in Jerusalem. That conversation lasted more than five hours, and I didn't want it to end! It was something that so deeply affected every part of my being, that, after I hugged her and said goodnight, I returned to the room I was sharing with three brothers, took a shower, and just lay down on my bed. I had no idea what to do with all that I had just experienced. I literally felt as though I had stepped into another dimension, and all I could do was try to express to God what was going on in my heart. To be honest, I couldn't even find words to convey how beautiful those five hours had been for me. I tried, but I couldn't. I just wept, thanked God, and asked Him for another opportunity to continue the conversation with her.

I simply had no idea that anything that indescribably, wonderfully beautiful could ever take place between two people in Him. I had always thought, wondered, and dreamed about it, and I dared to keep hoping for it. Yet, to be truthful, I was beginning to wonder if it was just a distant, possible dream. I was beginning to really question how, when, where, and with whom that could all ever possibly come together.

There are divine appointments which the Lord intends for His sovereign purposes that we know nothing about, unless He reveals something to us. As I walked down the passageway from the gate to board the plane which would take me to Jerusalem for that convocation that September, the Lord spoke deeply into my spirit, and said, *"You are standing on holy ground. You are connecting to My land and My people, and you are standing on holy ground!"* During that flight, He continued to speak into my spirit and informed me He had prepared divine appointments and meetings for me—that there would be many new contacts and doors of relationship and opportunity in Him.

In Jerusalem, the spiritual atmosphere is quite unlike any other place on earth. Things that would normally take weeks, months, or even years in the natural realm can take place through the Holy Spirit in just a few moments, minutes, or hours there in the City of the Great King. A sense of His glory is tangibly present in Jerusalem, particularly so at that annual convocation which brings together the nations to seek, honor and glorify God. It is a privilege to be there and participate at what many have called "God's United Nations." I experienced something of that glory dimension in an unforgettable way through that beautiful, life-changing, five-hour conversation.

I didn't sleep much that night. It was really a kind of all-night prayer and worship session with the Lord—perhaps the most significant one I have ever had. During those hours of time alone with Him in that room (my roommates were all in a very deep sleep), I had the sense that I was Adam, there in the garden, looking at Eve for the first time. I could truly feel something of what Adam must have felt. I thought, *Wow, I feel totally in love with her! I can't really believe my eyes when I see who You have fashioned here. She is just so beautiful! I don't even know what to do, where to begin, or how to approach her. Am I dreaming this, or is this reality? If it's a dream, I don't want to ever wake up! But if it's reality, I'd better figure out what to do, and do something quickly. Wow! Thank You, Lord! I had no idea You could come up with someone like this, like her. How did You do that? How did You know to fashion her so perfectly, so delightfully to my eyes and my whole being? You are amazing, Lord!*

Not only did I feel this overwhelming desire to share everything with her (Eve), I also felt that my whole life purpose and destiny were now forever linked with hers, and that everything I would do and say from that moment on would flow out of and depend on my conversation with her and with God.

What do you do with something like that? Who can you talk with about something like that, except to Him? You can't really discuss it with the other person, at least not yet, because you've only just met, and she might think you are really "out there." You don't want to be out there; you want to be right here, in the moment with her to continue the conversation. For you, however, the conversation will never be the same, because God has shown you a part of the profound mystery of who she really is in His eyes. What do you with that? Where do you put that, as you're trying to be the same person with her that you were the evening before at dinner? You are not the same person, because He's totally reset your heart, and nothing from that moment on will ever be as it had been for you. What do you do with all of that?

For me, it meant a lot of processing—a lot. Almost every night, for weeks after that, I processed—sometimes for half of the night, and it involved a lot of prayer, writing, tears, and communication with her. There were also a lot of emotional ups and downs, as I tried to figure out where she was and what was going on inside her heart, as well as inside mine.

Within one week of returning to Hungary from Jerusalem in late September 2018, the Lord gave me the idea—and commission—to write this book about marriage. He informed me the writing would be completed by that Christmas, which it was. This writing project was birthed over that five-hour dinner conversation in Jerusalem, and much of it flowed from the continuing conversation I shared with that beautiful, amazing daughter of the Most High God. This book and that ensuing three-month conversation are really one. There would have been no book without her and that continuing exchange of ideas and experiences after the convocation.

Let's go back now to Adam and Eve in the garden. In September 2018, the Lord gave me what I believe to be additional insight as to what happened in the Garden of Eden—why it went wrong, whose mistake it really was, and what we need to learn from this.

God created Adam first, and, because He did, Adam was given primary responsibility for the garden and for everything God had created. The Lord designed and fashioned Eve to be Adam's equal partner, but he was given responsibility to guard, watch over, and protect the garden. Adam was head of security. That was just one of his responsibilities but perhaps the most important one. He was to be alert and watchful, 24/7—ready and determined to confront and repel any kind of intruder attempting to trespass there. When that serpent broke in illegally, Adam should have intervened and cut that nasty snake's head off, instantly! If he had done so, the conversation the snake started with Eve would have never taken place, and everything would have remained the way God had originally created it.

Eve missed the mark here, as well. Why did she even listen to that other voice? She should have immediately shouted out to Adam, *"Adam! Come quickly! Intruder!"* Nevertheless, Adam failed on his watch; he wasn't doing his duty. Where was he at the moment the serpent stepped in? What was Adam doing? Did he fall asleep, or was he daydreaming about being with Eve later that night? I don't know, but he failed, and did so miserably! He let his guard down for a moment, and all of us have been paying an enormous price for his mistake ever since. Not only did we lose our innocent state of sinlessless and intimate fellowship with the Lord God, we also lost our ability to perfectly understand, effortlessly communicate with, and unselfishly relate to the opposite sex. We've been trying to hide from God and from each other and experiencing relationship and identity confusion ever since.

In the midst of that perfect world, something went wrong—horribly wrong. Someone started listening to the wrong messages. An intruder snuck into the garden and tried to engage Eve in the chat room which was only supposed to be between her, Adam, and the Lord. Suddenly, there was a predator on the loose, and that marauder was looking for a victim. He used charm and deceit to get Eve's attention, just the way modern-day internet predators try to snare their unsuspecting prey. Adam chose to believe the lies which that intruder spoke to Eve, rather than obey the instructions of the Lord not to eat of the fruit of the tree of the knowledge of good and evil.

The Lord showed me that, each time He begins to create something of strategic importance, the enemy will immediately look for a way to divert, distract, attack, derail, or destroy it. The attacks are likely to come at a time and in a way that we would least likely expect them. We already have complete victory in those battles through the blood of Yeshua, but we must be aware of the evil one's tactics, put on the whole armor of God, and be vigilant watchmen and women over our hearts and minds to prevent the enemy from gaining any kind of foothold.

I made the same mistake Adam did, because I didn't take the Lord's specific instructions to me seriously enough. Perhaps my negligence wasn't at the same level as Adam's dereliction of duty was, but it was just as serious, as I see it. In that sense, any one of us could have missed the mark, just as Adam did. Very early on the morning of September 19th, 2018, Yom Kippur, the Day of Atonement, the Lord awoke me and gave me this word:

"This new seed of creation, this new foundation that I have been planting and laying in you here in Jerusalem, will need to be sealed here in the covering of My blood (sacrifice on the cross) and holy Name before you leave. The enemy will come and attempt to steal, kill, and destroy what I have birthed in you. You must be a vigilant watchman on the walls of the garden,

which is your heart. Guard, protect, and nourish this precious treasure. Wash it daily in the transforming power of My eternal Word, so that it will grow up into the strong, majestic tree of My love and glory which I have purposed in you—from the very beginning—to be, shine, and bear bountiful fruit, and to be a testimony and manifestation of My salvation and goodness.

I have set you apart to manifest the tenderness and beauty of My heart and to be a model of what it truly means to walk joyfully, confidently, and victoriously as one—in holiness before Me.

I am your Source and all that you need. You are My beloved."

This is the word the Lord gave me that morning. I wrote it down into my small notebook and had planned to ask 'Eve' to pray with me and to seal it together in His blood and Word before we departed on a three-day prayer tour at the end of the convocation. I kept looking for the right moment to do that during the final meeting before departure but waited too long. Then, suddenly, it was time to board the bus and depart. I did pray that prayer alone later that morning, but it was only after we had left Jerusalem and the Lord had specifically instructed me to seal everything in prayer with her before leaving. I didn't take His instructions seriously enough, and because I didn't, a spiritual attack came later that morning in the form of a misunderstanding which resulted in a nearly total shutdown of my capacity to communicate with her for much of the rest of that day. I felt as if the precious gift of our friendship was quickly slipping away—forever, but felt powerless to change the situation, though I spent much of that day in prayer and declaring Scripture on the bus.

Finally, later that afternoon, the Lord spoke sternly to my spirit and showed me that this was a full-frontal attack by the enemy to drive a wedge between 'Eve' and me. He also told me that if I didn't immediately stand up, engage the adversary, take authority over the situation in His name, and take a step toward her to try to restart the conversation, the enemy would prevail. God showed me the seriousness of the situation and gave me the detemination to get in the fight and persevere until we had pushed back the adversary and reclaimed what he was trying to destroy. It was only by God's grace and mercy that 'Eve' and I could later that evening sit down, pray over, and share about what had happened and then move forward.

The lesson here is two-fold:

1. When the Lord gives you a very specific instruction, you should take it seriously, make it a priority, and not allow anyone or anything to prevent you from obeying Him as quickly as you can. He gave you that word for a specific purpose, and He is holding you accountable for that.

2. God has given men the responsibility to take the inititative to be spiritual servant leaders for their specific areas of influence and relationship. A man is called to be the spiritual priest of his home, workplace, and areas of influence—and, with great love, to minister to, pray for, lead, and serve all those for whom he is in some way responsible. If a man's wife is serving in a leadership capacity, he is called to stand with her, assist her, and be her primary source of spiritual, emotional, mental, and physical support.

For me, personally, Dave Meyer is a beautiful, powerful example of how this kind of ministry partnership in the Lord can, and should be lived out. Dave Meyer has sought to love, cherish, and support his wife, Joyce Meyer, in every way possible, so that she could grow and develop into the amazing, strong, influential woman of God she has become—with a global ministry impacting hundreds of millions of people. From what I see, Dave has consistently looked for ways to add value to his wife and their marriage. I would encourage all husbands to follow Dave Meyer's model of marital faithfulness, commitment, persistence, support, and encouragement, so that God can raise up all couples together to fulfill all that He desires to accomplish in and through them.

Both men and women of faith are equally called to be servant leaders and ministry partners, but the man is called to sacrificially set the example of what this looks like. Our Heavenly Father holds men accountable for how they handle this. A man who is not functioning fully in this capacity is negligent. The enemy will use that opening to attack that man's family, workplace, congregation, business, and all areas in which he is supposed to exercise servant leadership. I thank God for all of the dedicated, faithful men who are passionately engaged in all the Lord has called them to do, yet, there are far too many homes, ministries, workplaces, and communities around the world where the men of God are either absent, unaware, or only partially fulfilling their responsibility before the Lord to provide this essential spiritual example and protective covering.

I especially thank God for all of the beautiful, strong, amazing, resourceful, and committed women of faith all over the world who continuously seek and steadfastly follow the Lord in all of the areas where He has called them to serve. Sometimes, however, these precious sisters in the Lord are the only ones laboring where they are, because there are no men present to work alongside them. God is calling each one of us to seek Him about our true calling and to completely step into that, so that His body is functioning at full capacity and effectiveness for the advancement of His kingdom, of which there shall be no end. We need strong, healthy, vibrant models of men and women of faith working and serving God together: fully honoring, encouraging, empowering, and supporting each other in all communities of the world, so that people can see living examples of this equal partnership.

As He calls, equips, and sends us, God is also in the process of restoring us to the Garden—the place of deep intimacy between man and woman joined together in His love—the place where He walks with us daily as His presence and glory abound and transform us into His image.

Let us enter in together to receive, declare, experience, and give thanks for all that He has purposed for us, to His eternal glory and praise forevermore. Amen!

Chapter 2: What If

This chapter is about the what-if's of life, especially those regarding matters of the heart.

Before we begin, I don't think it's advisable to spend too much time in the discontinued items bin of the what-if department of the shopping mall of life. Those things are from our past, and going there without the specific purpose of understanding and healing those experiences will only bring regret, self-condemnation, and disappointment. Let's not even go there, unless the Holy Spirit is conducting a search and rescue mission of that sector and wants to do something in that for our edification and sanctification.

As for exploring the what-if's which pertain to our present or our future? Absolutely! You'd better believe that's okay, because that's the only place we're going to find the right questions to help us discover where God is in our life at the moment, what He's doing, and what He's inviting us to participate in with Him next. One of the things I believe He's especially keen on is helping us discover what's really going on in our heart.

Let's face it: one of the biggest problems we have in life is that we don't really know our own heart; we don't. Sometimes, we think we do, but, even then, what we think we understand is only a tiny piece of a marvelously intricate system which speaks a very different language from the one our conscious, logical mind uses for communication. Come to think of it, much of the time, when our heart is speaking or trying to talk to us, we fail to even recognize it. The heart doesn't shout; it whispers. It can be all too easy to miss it when it's trying to get our attention, especially when our daily lives are so full of background, social media, societal, and internal noise. Yes, I am recommending that we turn a lot more of that stuff off and tune in to the voice of the Holy Spirit much more often if we want to hear something of importance, because that's the only way it's going to happen.

Let's be honest: if we're spending four hours daily on social media and only giving God a half hour a day, we're not even giving Him equal, let alone priority, time. It's not even close. How would you feel if your future wife or husband did that to you? I can hear some of you saying, *"Divorce court, for committing adultery!"* God hates divorce; He wants couples to discuss and agree on issues like this long before they walk down the aisle and say *"I do."*

The other problem is, even if we hear what our heart is saying, we are often not in a place where we even have the time or capacity to deal with it. We might have heard something, but we just file it away in a folder for future reference. A lot of times, the message just gets buried among all of the other miscellaneous bits of information that arrived in our in-box that day, so the chances of our finding it again and doing something with it are slim—really slim. A worst case scenario would be that we glance at it, mistakenly think it's spam or junk mail, and quickly delete it. The good news here is the Holy Spirit has total access to all of our files, even the deleted or trash ones. If there is something really important related to our prophetic destiny that we've missed, He can go back, retrieve it, and bring it to our attention, if we're listening.

Finding Ms. or Mr. Right

I am of the opinion that God must have one ideally matched covenant partner for each of us. When He helps us find that person, He will work through us to transform one other in order to create the best possible marriage for the specific purpose that He has intended. He knows each of us perfectly, and He sees everything. After He saves us, calls us to Himself, and we begin following Him, isn't it up to Him to show us that person or introduce them to us? Isn't that far better than us trying to find that person by ourself? There could be several hundred million possibilities out there to choose among, and how in the world could any of us really have any idea who we should be looking for? Without the Lord guiding and arranging the process, it really is like looking for a needle in a haystack.

How do we know, and how can we recognize that special someone when He introduces or presents them to us? Is it possible to miss him or her? How do we know that they will also recognize us? Is there any guarantee that both of us will be on the same wavelength when we meet, or that we will have enough time and ample opportunity to get to know each other well enough to discern and decide whether or not the Lord is really in that process, as well as to find out how we really feel about that person? With the increased mobility of people in the world today, just being in the same place together for a long enough period of time can, in itself, be a real challenge. God knows all of the details, and He knows what He is doing. Our task is to keep seeking Him: to listen, wait, watch, pray, trust, declare, stand, receive, thank, and act while we are in the process of discovering who He has called us to share our life together with in Him.

One of the most difficult aspects of seeking our wife or husband is waiting. Most of the time, we really just want to arrive—to find her or him and begin the mysterious, amazing journey of this "two becoming one." We don't want to spend a lot of time in the search process, because we're focused on the destination. The process, however, is where God is doing the most work and preparation, so that we will be ready for the right person when He presents her or him to us. Sometimes, the search and waiting process turns out to be a whole lot longer than we would have liked. For some, it seems like it will never end. *"Where is this person, Lord? Do you really have someone just for me? Have you forgotten about me and what I asked You many years ago?"*

What happens when we do meet someone in the Lord, and we have a strong sense or even a word from Him that *"this is the one"*? What happens when we think we've received that message and begin to unpack it, but the other person hasn't gotten that same word or revelation? Did we make a mistake? Did we pick up a signal meant for someone else and think it was for us, or did we really hear something from the Lord? Sometimes it can be very confusing and frustrating to try and sort all of this out.

What happens when the other person also heard something from God about us but feels that they're not ready, or they're unwilling to step toward us, or they just have issues that we know nothing about? What if we're the one who isn't ready, who is unwilling to step toward them, or we have issues the other person knows nothing about which prevent us from taking a step closer?

Now we're getting into some really fascinating territory here, because we have two very different spirit-beings: one male and one female—both with a free will; both with a separate way of perceiving and experiencing reality, which could be the subject of a book in and of itself; both with a different family background and formation, and both with a radically different type of CPU/brain processor.

When we put all of this together, we're suddenly facing lots of variables, a number of possibilities, and many things that could go very well or very badly in the communication process. Where is God in all of that? Well, He's definitely in it; I know He is. It appears that He likes complexity, and, at times, perhaps even a tiny measure of ambiguity to go along with it. My advice is to just embrace it, and most importantly, *to embrace Him* in the midst of it. In other words, just try to enjoy the journey, and quit trying to figure it all out. First of all, you can't, and second of all, if you try to make logical sense of it, you'll just end up feeling frustrated, confused, and disappointed. Besides, who ever said the process would or should be an easy one? To quote a great line from a marvelous short film, *"The greater the struggle, the more glorious the triumph!"*[1]

Is it possible that there could be more than one potential "Ms. or Mr. Right?" If that is so, where is the heart of God in all of that? Is He really the Divine Matchmaker? Is He still in the business of drawing two hearts together and helping them find each other, or is that just a romantic fairy tale that has no basis in reality? So, if God really is the Divine Matchmaker, how does He operate in this wonderfully mysterious, complex dance of one human heart longing for and seeking another? He is the One who put this yearning in us, so it's a beautiful and precious thing to Him, and I believe He wants us to experience it that way.

It really gets back to this mysterious question of how it all works: God's plan for our life, our choices, His will, and our destiny. It's a huge mystery, and if someone says they have a formula to explain how all of this plays out, I would say, *No, you don't. You have no idea. Only God knows, and He's the only one who can give us revelation about this.* What I do know for certain is that He is very intentional about everything and everyone that He permits, arranges, and presents to us. He always has a purpose, even if we can't or don't see it, and that purpose is *Jeremiah 29:11*. It's all there.

Because He knows where each person is right at each moment, He can see who is open, who is ready, who is not, and who wants to take the next step in Him toward that other person. What is more, I think He is in that process to help both persons identify where they are, what they truly desire in a relationship, and what potential and possibilities they recognize in that other person. Even when one person perceives something in the other and sees that God is doing something, but the other person doesn't sense that or only does so to a lesser extent, the Lord is still working in that to bring both people closer to Him and to what He really desires for them. If they're ready and willing to take that significant step of commitment toward each other, then He can begin to create something gloriously beautiful, as He prepares them for their unique mission of service to Him as a married couple. Again, I have no idea how He does all of this, because He is sovereign, and His purposes are often hidden—only to be revealed at a later time.

I think it all comes down to what He showed me in October 2018 during an English class with my freshman 9A group at Horváth Mihály Gimnázium: ***"See the Potential! Show the Possibilities! Inspire toward Perfection!"***

It's all right there in a nutshell, in these three simple expressions—however, He is asking each of us to unpack it. God doesn't just hand us a finished product, He presents us with possibilities and opportunities which are often disguised as problems or crises. Very often, we fail to even recognize that what He's really doing is offering us an amazing opportunity—sometimes even the chance of a lifetime!

The Lord has shown me that some doors of invitation or opportunity in Him may come with an expiration date. This means that there may be a set amount of time given for us to recognize the significance of those divine appointment moments and to step into or through them when they are being offered. If we miss those appointed times, those doors may close—sometimes forever. The Lord may very well open other doors to us but perhaps not those same ones again. I experienced that myself. I missed a huge door of opportunity many years ago, because I waited too long to express what was in my heart toward someone, and then, when I did, it was already too late. That door suddenly closed in front of me, and it never reopened. It took me many years to make peace with that mistake and loss, but now I can thank Him for all that He did allow me to experience before that happened, and for what He has taught me through that experience.

We need to ask the Lord for discernment, so that we can clearly see when He is opening an important door of opportunity to us and what that means. It is essential that we be paying attention: that we be listening, receptive, responsive, obedient, and prepared for these unexpected times of visitation or presentation. Our entire future and destiny will be shaped and decided by how attentive and responsive we are to Him when He is moving in our lives.

Thou hast dealt well with Thy servant,
O Lord, according to Thy word.
Teach me good discernment and knowledge,
For I believe in Thy commandments. (Psalm 119:65–66 NASB)

Chapter 3: Boxes

God desires to show up in our everyday lives and manifest Himself. He is sovereign, and it's His choice as to when, where, and how He will do something. Much of the time, we aren't really expecting Him to appear, or, if we are, we expect He will move exactly the way He did the last time. It's possible He will, but usually God does the next thing differently from the way He did the previous one. He never changes, but His approach, methods, and strategies can vary. From what I have observed, He seems to enjoy doing new things in fresh, unexpected ways. He is completely out-of-the box, and He wants us to learn to be out-of-the-box as well.

Most of us try to make sense of our life, situations, and relationships by putting everything and everyone into different kinds of boxes. This situation is this type of box. That over there, that's another type of box, and that person, they're definitely a third kind of box. We like to categorize and compartmentalize people and things; it's one of the ways we try to organize everything so we can better understand life. We keep trying to put God into some kind of box, too—as though we could actually figure Him out or how He does things. He is God; He is way too big for any box to contain Him. He can't and won't limit Himself to our tiny understanding of who He is and how He operates. He's much too big for any of that, so let's please stop trying to fit Him into a box! *Forget the boxes! Get rid of them! Stay out of them!*

Here is one of the major problems people who do not believe in God have with believers: they don't understand our church and denomination boxes. They can't fathom how God could possibly exist in these miniscule structures that we have created, or how we can claim to present Him as fitting into those. That just doesn't make any sense to a lot of people who are outside, looking in. They're searching for God, at least some of them are, but we're presenting them with boxes. It's no wonder so many of our church services and buildings are almost empty. How can people possibly find God in something created by human hands? They can't, so they continue to look elsewhere—those who are truly searching.

If we would just let God out of our boxes and let Him be **GOD**, people would be lining up at our doors, trying to get in. Where the Spirit of the Lord is welcome in His fullness and glory, people are seeing God reveal Himself and are being touched by the tangible, heavy, very real presence of the Most High God. This is starting to happen all over the world now, and it's the beginning of the third Pentecost, just as prophesied through the prophet Joel:

"And it will come about after this that I will pour our My Spirit on all mankind; And your sons and daughters will prophesy, Your old men will dream dreams, Your young men will see visions." (Joel 2:28 NASB)

This outpouring is going to be tremendously glorious, and we have the extraordinary privilege of preparing ourselves for Him to come and reveal Himself. He doesn't need our help to be who He is. He does wait to be invited, though. We have to make room for Him and create a space: a place in our hearts where He is truly welcome—a place of hospitality. First, however, we've got to rid of these boxes—all of them—they simply have to go!

Why is out-of-the-box so important? I have been thinking about this a lot since the 2018 Jerusalem Convocation and asking the Lord to help me understand this. When we are in boxes, it is very difficult for God to get in and to show us new things, because we are filtering everything through the lens of our box mindset. That lens can only focus on one narrow thing at a time, and He is infinite, so we limit what He can reveal to us and do through us. God always has much more for us than we could ever imagine and is waiting for us to take a step closer to Him, so He can release what He has prepared for us.

A relationship with a box is not very fulfilling; predictable, yes—but satisfying? Not in the least! A box is designed to hold or contain a certain amount of something, and when the box is full, that's it. There isn't any more room in that box to contain anything. Do you see what I'm getting at here? A box doesn't have the ability to expand or add volume; it's limited. God designed people to embody and express something of Himself. He's unlimited and so is the potential He has placed within us, if we are seeking Him in all areas of our life. When we put somebody into a box, what we are really saying to them is: *"This is all you are. This is all you're ever going to be—right here—what's visible in this box. You don't have any more potential. This is it; this is your limit!"* How would you feel if someone said that to you? Has anyone ever spoken to you that way? Have you ever said that to someone else or even to yourself? All too often, we focus much more on what is missing, either in ourself or in another person, and we fail to recognize what is there. That too is a kind of boxed-in thinking which limits what we can see and appreciate.

Boxes are very useful for storing things. We put stuff we don't have room for or don't know what to do with into a box, and we place that carton onto a shelf. The only problem is, we forget what we have placed in that box. We rarely, if ever, get around to unpacking, examining, and deciding what to do with its contents. They continue to just sit there; unused and unemployed. We can easily do that with people, too; we put them into a box, stick them onto a shelf, and forget about them. They just sit there, gathering dust.

We even do that with ourself. We put our talents and abilities, especially the ones we never have time or energy to do anything with, and we put those into a box and place it onto a shelf, for later. All too often, later means too late, which tragically results in wasted talent, undeveloped abilities, and missed destinies. All we needed to do was to go over to that shelf, dust off that box, open it, take another look at its contents, and make a decision about what to do with it. All of that promising, potential talent can so easily be forgotten, unharnessed, and lost forever, simply because of inattention or neglect. What an unimaginable loss it is when that occurs!

Please go back and read *Matthew 25:14–29*, the parable of the talents, and you'll see how serious an issue this is with the Lord. He asks that we use what He has entrusted to us wisely and fruitfully. This responsibility begins with our faith, which is paramount to all of the other things He has given to us to be productive stewards over. God doesn't waste resources, and He expects us to commit all that we have to Him and put it to maximum use as He guides and directs us. He is the Dream-Giver, Resource Provider, and Project Manager of all that we are given to accomplish.

I've always loved the story of Abraham and his journey. God met him right where he was, revealed Himself, and blessed him with an astounding promise. Then, His first instruction to him was to leave everything and everyone, take his wife Sara and a few servants, and go out, not knowing where he was going. That was a pretty radical calling; to leave and not have any idea where he was being sent. What would I do if the Lord asked me to do that? I know I would want to obey, but would I really? Do I have the faith for that kind of leap? I know He has given each of us a measure of faith, but would I be willing to activate what He has already deposited in me and take that giant stride out into the unknown? I really don't know; I would want to, but would I? Would you?

Why did God do that? Was it really necessary? Couldn't He have just taught Abraham right where he was, little by little? Would that have worked? Sometimes, the only way God can show us new things and bring us into the destiny He has for us is to take us out of where we are—out of our comfort zone—and relocate us. This is what He did with me when I first came here to Hungary many years ago. I thought it was just a great adventure: a rare opportunity to experience life where there had been a very closed and repressive system, just as it was opening up, and to hopefully contribute something positive to its rebirth.

I believe that was a small part of what God wanted to do in me at that time, but, as I look back on those experiences now, I see that He needed a period of years to extract me from the boxes I had been living and thinking in, to introduce new truths from His Word, and to establish His ways in my heart. Today, He continues to challenge me to jettison the new boxes of limitation I have constructed for myself and others since then. The following dream and interpretation bear witness of His desire to help us break free of all limiting mindsets.

The Dream

I'm outside. Suddenly, I see that my dog, Zsemi, is out in the middle of the street, and he's chasing a bird—in fact, several birds. I run after him and see a car coming. Thankfully, the driver sees Zsemi, slows down, and avoids hitting him, but Zsemi keeps running—still chasing those birds. He loves running after things. I keep running after him, shouting his name, and trying to get him to stop chasing the birds and come back, because I'm worried another car might come suddenly.

Then, I see him chasing a bird inside a large swimming pool. The bird flies toward the water, Zsemi jumps into the air after the bird, and then plunges into the water, where he's still trying to catch it. I keep calling to him, but he doesn't pay any attention: he's totally focused on following that bird. I step out of that indoor swimming pool area for a second and see another, larger pool outside which looks very appealing. The whole area around the pool is full of people lying and relaxing on lounge chairs. Nobody's in the water, though, which is strange. I feel like getting in the water and swimming. It's a perfect time to have the pool all to myself.

After that, I'm back at the place where I'm living, and the door is ajar. I left it open when I ran out after Zsemi, so he could get back in. I step inside and walk through the living space. It's not clear whether it's a house or an apartment. As I walk through, I see that the furniture which I think belongs to my housemate, the person who has been renting that living space with me, is gone. It looks like someone came in and just removed or stole it. My first thought is to call the housemate and tell them the furniture is gone, but I don't do that. I keep walking through the miniscule rooms. Each tiny space is connected by a very narrow L-shape. As I walk through, I even get lost for a moment, because the way the tiny spaces are connected is really disorienting. Finally, I make my way into the main room, and, as I walk into it, I'm shocked at how tiny it is! I feel extremely claustrophobic just looking at it! As I'm staring at it, I wonder how in the world I could have ever lived in that cramped space. There's barely enough room for one person, and actually there's not enough. I love spacious rooms and hate small spaces. All I want to do at that moment is get out of there, so I immediately start to exit. I can't wait to escape! Then, suddenly, I'm out! Freedom! A huge sigh of relief! I know for certain that I never want to go back into that tiny space again!

Then, I wake up. I wonder what the dream is all about. I ask the Lord to help me understand what this dream means and what He wants to show me here.

The Dream Interpretation

That tiny house or apartment looks nothing like my house, the one I'm living in now, so I know that building in the dream is not my real house; it's my inner house or residence. And Zsemi? It could be Zsemi, but here I'm pretty sure Zsemi is something or someone else. I think Zsemi is a specific person in real life. The bird is a dove, and the dove represents the Holy Spirit, which suggests this specific person is intent on chasing after or following the Holy Spirit with all of their focus and attention.

Then, the Lord says to me in my spirit: "The house and the rooms you've been living in are too small! You can't fit there. You can't even live there anymore. There's not even enough room for you and certainly not enough for anyone else! That's why you ran out. You knew you didn't fit there any longer. Let Me enlarge the rooms of your house, which is your heart.

Let Me make them larger—more spacious! I can do that, if you'll let Me. You can't live in that tiny inner space any longer. There's no room there for anyone else, either. You need more space! Lots more space! Let Me add space to your residence! Tons of space!

And let that specific other person out of the tiny space, the box you've been putting them into! Let them out! They can't fit there! I didn't design them to fit there! They don't fit, and they're not supposed to fit into your tiny box for them! Stop it! Let them out of the box!

I created them to feel and enjoy the total freedom in Me that they want and need. That is what they are looking for and what they are finding in Me. That's what I want for you as well: just total freedom in Me—no boxes—not for them— not for you! Get rid of the boxes! Find your freedom in Me."

Now, you might be thinking, as I have at times, *"That sounds great, but if I invite Him to come and remove all of these boxes, once and for all, what will happen then? I won't have any place left to hide!"* And now, I hear the Lord saying in response:

"Exactly! No more place to hide! Fully open, fully exposed, fully vulnerable, and fully free; in Me! Just as it was in

the very beginning, when Adam and Eve both walked naked in the garden and were not ashamed (Genesis 2:25). Total purity—total innocence—fellowship—unity—delight—joy—trust—ecstasy—total power of the purpose of a man and a woman together(what the enemy fears most and why he tries to destroy marriages)—in harmony; with Me! Wow! And you want to stay in those boxes?"

Maybe you've put God into a box by thinking He should have done something you were asking or expecting from Him in a certain way, but He didn't. Maybe you asked Him to give you something in a particular manner, at a specific time when you thought it should have been there. Maybe God didn't show up and meet your expectations, whatever those were, in the exact way or timing you thought He should have. Perhaps you have blamed God for a loss in your life, or you think He is punishing you or treating you unfairly.

There are so many ways we can, and do put God into a box of our own creation. In fact, we do this every single day, and most of the time we aren't even aware of it. We try to create Him "in our own image," to make Him fit into our own limited ways of thinking, feeling, and expectation. We keep trying to squeeze Him into our narrow frames of reference and experience, but He is not there, in those boxes, and He never will be. His thoughts are far above what we think and how we see and comprehend things.

If we are ever to understand something about what God is really doing and desires to do in and through us, we will need to empty ourself, be immersed daily in His Word, and be attentive and still before Him, so the Holy Spirit can speak to us. We need fresh revelation from Him about who He is and what His heart desires, so we can align ourselves with His purposes and flow in harmony with Him in every area of our life. **This means total surrender.** This means raising the white flag. It means letting go of all of our limited perceptions of who He is and how He operates—then asking Him to fill us with Himself.

Just as the Lord exhorted me to do in that dream, let us all make the decision today to step out of all the boxes we have created for ourselves, to let other people out of the boxes we have placed them in, and to forget about ever trying to put God into a box. Then, as He directs, let us take all of our man-made cartons, shred them into tiny pieces, and let us step out boldly together into the fullness of the glorious freedom and destiny He has purposed for each one of us. Let us find our freedom, our total freedom, in Him.

If therefore the Son shall make you free, you shall be free indeed. (John 8:36 NASB)

Chapter 4: The Storyteller

God, the Master Storyteller, loves good stories. No one can even begin to tell a story like He can. If you think about it, as you read the Bible, the living Word of the living God, you will discover that all of human history is really about His story: the creation; His calling out a special people to represent Him; how He interacted with them; His sending His Son, Jesus, to model how we are to live; His Son taking on Himself the suffering and penalty for all our sin, and His Son resurrecting from the dead in order to restore everything that had been lost.

Human history is the story of the loving Father who treasures us so much, that He was willing to pay the ultimate price to save us—the loving Father who never gives up on us and pursues us passionately with His love.

That's why it's so important to read, study, sit with, meditate on, declare, and pray over His written Word to us, the Holy Scriptures. Those words are God-breathed and annointed; written by men, yes, but inspired by His Holy Spirit. They are His timeless message to us. His Words carry life and contain everything we need to know for our own lives.

Amazingly, He is also keenly interested in our personal stories, and He longs to create new adventures in, with, and through us. Every day with the Lord is story time. He is always doing something new, fresh, unexpected, and wonderful. God really wants us to enter in to each day's story in Him with childlike faith, enthusiasm, and expectancy. That pleases Him greatly!

Did you know that there are books in Heaven's Library about your life—about what the Father imagined and dreamed about you from the very beginning—about what He, you, and others could do together? Did you know that? Have you ever wondered what is written on the pages of the books about you in Heaven's Library? You can ask Him to reveal to you what He wants you to know about the destiny and perfect plans He has for your life.

God wants to create great life stories with and through us: stories that reflect His goodness, glory, and the best of who we can become through the course of our life journey. He wants our life story to become a great example and an inspiration to those around us who are looking for direction but haven't yet discovered that their true purpose can only be found in Him.

While He was on earth in human form, Jesus was a Master Storyteller. When we read the accounts in the New Testament of the stories and parables He shared with His disciples and the crowds who gathered to listen to Him, we can sense something of the creative tension that must have been present in the hearts and minds of His audience, as they hung on His every word.

He always made sure the examples He used were relevant and easily understood by the common people to whom He was talking; He communicated with them at their level. That's what a good teacher does: he or she presents the material in a clear, culturally relevant, and compelling way. Sometimes, he or she informs, sometimes questions, sometimes challenges, sometimes encourages, and sometimes corrects. It's all part of the process. He or she always tries to be a good model and guide. Sometimes, a good teacher has a personal word or question for the student to help them through a difficult period or to inspire them to take a step toward their good future.

If you've ever heard His voice, either in your own spirit or audibly, you know that every word He speaks is life, and that just a single word or question from Him can alter the course of your life. Just one life-giving word of His can do that.

He asked me four questions one night in Jerusalem that September, and those questions began to change the direction of my entire future. Those four questions, in effect, reset my entire life path, and, through them, God invited me to step into a deeper dimension of heart intimacy with Him and toward another person. Those four questions were: *"Do you see it? Do you see the hidden treasure here? Do you see her? Do you see (the person's name)?"*

A master teacher always has just the right questions to put to his students: questions that make them really think or even cause some discomfort. It isn't enough to just impart knowledge and wisdom, as important as those are. The best teachers understand the importance of inviting those studying with them to think more deeply about what they are being taught: to examine, process, reflect on, and take to heart the lessons in that material.

Knowledge and wisdom are only half of the package, however. Wisdom teaches us what knowledge really means, but it is only as we begin to activate what we have learned that we start to experience its power and ability to bring about positive transformation. If we don't harness and put into practice what we learn, it remains passive and unexpressed. We need all three: knowledge, wisdom, and application. Time is required in order to acquire and activate all of that—yes, time.

Time in our modern world is a precious commodity. There are always countless tasks and responsibilities on our daily to-do lists. God wants us to take our duties seriously, yet, at the same time, He reminds us that our first and primary assignment is to listen to Him. Listening requires time, demands focus, and necessitates reprioritizing our daily activities.

There are seasons of constant, intense activity and tasks that have to be accomplished within a set time frame. God knows and understands that, and He stands ready to help us in those stressful periods. He wants us to do our very best, and He anoints everything He has called us to do for Him as we commit and dedicate it to Him. God wants the fruit of our labor and the products of our hands to be an excellent testimony about Him.

Yet, let us also remember that Jesus was never in a hurry; He always had time for what was most important. He was always listening to the voice of His Father, and He regularly retreated from the crowds and the busyness around Him to focus on what the Father was saying and asking Him to do next. Jesus is our example. He made sure He was constantly in perfect harmony with the Father, so He could be attending to just the right task or person, at just the right time, in order to complete the mission He came to fulfill.

God is inviting each of us today to give Him all the details of our own life story, especially the ones that don't fit anywhere or make any sense. He has a purpose and a plan, even in those. He is asking us right now to just listen, trust, and follow Him. He is inviting us to take the next step He has prepared for us and to keep moving forward with Him, so we can complete every part of the marvelous mission He has assigned to us: to be His loving hands and heart to all those around us. That's the story He wants to write with us on the pages of our hearts and lives: His story, within which ours is expressed. It's the best story out there, it really is. You don't want to miss it!

And He began to teach again by the seashore. And such a very great multitude gathered before Him that He got into a boat in the sea and sat down; and all the multitude were by the seashore on the land. And He was teaching them many things in parables . . . (Mark 4:1–2 NASB)

Chapter 5: Seeing Is Believing

We know that "believing is seeing" is how the principle of faith operates. God asks us to exercise faith in order to call the things that He has promised us, which already exist in the spiritual realm, from there into the physical world. For some, however, it is impossible to believe unless they first see physical evidence. After His resurrection, when Jesus appeared to His disciples, Thomas said that he would only believe it was really Jesus if he saw in His hands the imprint of the nails, put his finger into the place of the nails, and put his hand into Jesus' side. Only after he had done that was Thomas convinced it really was the resurrected Lord.

Jesus said to him, "Because you have seen Me, have you believed. Blessed are they who did not see, and yet believed." (John 20:29 NASB)

When God shows us something, when He allows us to really see something or someone with His eyes—from His perspective—He's really giving us an amazing gift: He's transferring to us His sense of sight. When we receive His forgiveness and Lordship and enter His eternal family and kingdom, He begins to give us a new type of eyesight. Before we received Him, we could only perceive and see things from a natural perspective with our visual physical sense organ, our eyes. That was the only way we were able to recognize things. We were also born with a measure of intuition, a possible sixth sense, which helps us perceive things which we can't see with our eyes, but here we're looking at a much greater and higher sensory scale than that: *the God level.*

As the Lord begins to transform us through our reading, studying, investigating, internalizing, believing, and applying His Word, which is all of Scripture, He also begins to sanctify our physical senses. Why does He do that? First of all, our five physical senses, as wonderful and important as they are, can currently only pick up sensory signals in this earthly realm, which is their intended area of function. God has marvelously designed and created each of these sensory organs in such a miraculous way so that they would function and serve His intended purpose. Everything He does is with perfect intention. These physical senses are not capable, because of our fallen natural state, of picking up signals and information from the heavenly realm.

Just as He gives us new life, which is Himself, and His Holy Spirit, He also breathes into our senses and sanctifies them so they can function at a much higher level and receive what He wants to show us. Personally, I think He is always sending something or sharing something with us, but are we tuned in and receptive? If your radio is connected to a power source, turned on, has a strong enough receiver, is tuned to a particular frequency, and there is no interference, the programs and information being broadcast through that signal will reach you. The question is, are you listening, paying attention, and expecting to hear something important? Are you in a state of constant receptivity and preparation to receive something new?

The world we live in today is a place filled with distractions. We're surrounded by noise: news of both the real and fictitious kinds; entertainment; trivial pursuits—you can make your own list here of the trivia in your life that so easily pull you from things that really matter; social media—great when used for important communication and to advance His kingdom, but not so useful when used for silly, self-centered, empty, or temporal things; computer games; destructive addictions, and many other things that pull us away from what is of importance to God and should therefore be to us as well.

In an atmosphere like this, where God is also constantly speaking to us through His still, small voice and the heavenly signals He is sending both to our spirit and to our senses, it can be extremely difficult for us to receive what He is trying to communicate to us. The problem isn't on His end; it's on ours. His signals are always crystal clear, but all too often our radio isn't even switched on. That's something that greatly grieves the Father's heart. He has so much more to share with us, but we're not even taking it seriously enough to tune in. How in the world will it ever be possible for us to step more deeply into all that He longs to do through us if our receiver is switched off?

Perhaps our radio is on, but it's tuned to the wrong station—not His frequency, but another. Who are we really listening to out there? There are people and situations that the Lord will speak to us through—in fact, many—but He also gives us discernment to recognize which voices are really from Him, and which are not. He wants to help us avoid being drawn into perceptions, opinions, and ideas which do not reflect truth.

He wants to protect us from everything, including people, who, even with good intentions on their part, are quick to give us their two cents(sometimes a whole dollar!) and more. I must confess, when someone starts to say something to me and immediately I sense in my spirit that it is not from the Lord, that it's from that person's own opinions or another source that isn't of God, I instantly begin looking for a polite way to change the topic of conversation or to disengage from it. I don't want to be pulled off course from what He has shown me to be true in His Word and confirmed by His Holy Spirit.

Our Heavenly Father really desires that we all be on the same page, and the page I am talking about here is not yours, mine, or ours: it's His. The Lord gets to write the story of each of our lives, because He is the One who imagined, designed, fashioned, and created each of us to reflect Him. He wants us to partner with Him and with each other in such amazing and glorious adventures, that we cannot even begin to imagine what they could be. Most of the time we are just seeing, thinking, and living small, when God is saying to us, *"Think big!"* God is not small: He's huge, infinite, and glorious!

Here's a staggering number about the design of the human brain from Dr. Caroline Leaf: *"You truly are unlimited—your brain has three million years plus worth of space."* If you meditate on that for a few minutes, you'll see that what we're beginning to talk about here is really eternity. That's something I can't even begin to get a handle on: without end—forever—never-ending. What is that? How does that work? We're stepping onto God territory here—into the supernatural quality of our Creator which surpasses huge, gigantic, colossal, and monumental. God is infinite, boundless, astronomical, inexhaustible, unfathomable, and utterly beyond human description and comprehension. Yet, He loves us and longs for us to be in continuous communion with Him.

I used to think about and refer to God as being first, or number one in my life. I always thought that was the best way to express this and that this was the proper way to talk about Him, but I was wrong. The Lord has shown me that *He is in a league of His own.* If we say that God is first, or number one, that implies that He is close to the same level as other things or persons in our lives, but is that really how it is? Can we, dare we try to compare Him to everyone and everything else?

God is in His own category: He cannot be likened to anything or anyone else, because everything and everyone in this universe was imagined, designed, and created by Him. To be honest, I haven't yet found a single word that can even begin to express this truth. I don't have an adequate expression with which to convey the fact that He is in a league of His own; human language fails me here. God is too big, too glorious, too awesome, too wonderful, too beautiful, and too majestic for any words of our human tongues to describe.

I believe it is appropriate that we consider using capital letters when we refer to GOD. It's a sign of respect for all that He is. We should look for ways to honor Him and try to express to Him that which is beyond our ability to describe or understand. We ought to be careful how we use words when we're talking about or referring to God, however, because it's easy to adopt a tone of what I call, "disrespectful familiarity," toward Him. Yes, He is our loving Abba and our Heavenly Daddy, but He is also the Great I AM, the Lord God Jehova, the Alpha and the Omega, Righteous Judge, and King! He deserves all of our attention, worship, praise, and adoration, because He alone is holy.

Let's determine in our hearts to tune in, every moment of every day; to listen for His voice and to be sensitive to His direction. He wants to share so much more with us about many things, but He will never force His way in. We have to make room for Him and invite Him to speak to us. May the Lord grant us hearts and senses which are fully open to Him: ready and eager to receive all that He desires to communicate to us.

Make room, make ready, and make time—invite Him in. If we do this continuously, we will begin to hear His voice more frequently, and we'll step into a deeper, more intimate dimension of fellowship and communion with God. That's what He longs for: a deeper relationship with us on all levels. Let's press in closer, listen more attentively, and pursue Him more intentionally. He is waiting.

Behold, I stand at the door and knock; if any one hears My voice and opens the door, I will come in to him, and will dine with him, and he with Me. (Revelation 3:20 NASB)

Chapter 6: A Place in His Heart

Early one morning this past October, as I was wrestling about something that wasn't right in my heart, confessing my brokenness before God, and asking Him to forever remove everything in me that isn't pleasing to Him, He allowed me, for a few brief minutes, to enter into the secret place of His heart, the Father's heart. I was invited to see, feel, and touch something of what He experiences there.

There is a place hidden deep within the innermost parts of our being: a place designed by Him, which He refers to as, *"the heart room."* This is a place that most of us don't visit very often, but it is the place out of which He desires for us to live every moment of our life. It is in this room where He longs to meet us: to show us who He is, to embrace us, to reassure us of His love and tenderness, and to let us just soak in all that He is and to enjoy His presence. Jesus is always standing there, just outside the door of our heart room, waiting for us to open it and invite Him in. It is a room that He designed and created just for Himself. It is a space that we often try to fill with other things, even other people, but they don't and they can't fit there. This room wasn't designed to be filled by them, only by Him.

As He began to show me a small part of His heart—His beautiful, tender heart—I said to Him:

I didn't know. I thought I knew, but I had no idea—none whatsoever. Please forgive me! I thought I knew what love, what Your love is, but I had no idea until this moment, here in Your heart, what it is. I have experienced it before; I have felt it before; I have received it before from You and from others, but I didn't understand it. I thought I did, but I really didn't. I realized what the words meant, and because of that, I thought I understood what love is—but I didn't. Forgive me.

This is what He showed me this morning: love is a decision. It is a choice from the freedom of our heart which is made willingly, longingly, without reservation, without conditions, and made without a sense of duty or obligation. Love simply says, *"I choose you above all others. I want you above all others. I desire you above all others. I willingly and wholeheartedly abandon all else and all others before you. You are the one—the only one I choose. I want no other but you—only you."*

This is love. This is how the Father loves us. He chooses to love us freely, willingly, longingly, without reservation, and without conditions. This is how He offers His love to us. We are free to receive or to reject His love. We are at liberty to share or to refuse to pass on His love to others. We are free to walk or to not walk in His love. It's a choice each moment of every day: a decision to remain in and live out of His love, or to ignore it and live life our own way, independently of Him.

It is what we choose every moment of each day that determines who we become. We decide if we will become more like Him, or if we will ignore Him and miss all that He longs to share with us, show us, and shower us with. It's a moment-by-moment choice: one which is completely in our hands.

I said to the Lord this morning: *I want only You. I choose only You. Forgive me for the countless times I have chosen something or someone else over You. Forgive me for the many occasions I have wanted and started to go my own way. I ask You—I beg You to completely annihilate everything in me that wants to go my own way and disregard You. I surrender my desire to be independent of You. I need You, I want You and I only desire to live my life in Your love. I don't want to live anywhere else or in any other way. Help me, Lord! Thank you for sharing Your heart with me and for teaching me what I didn't know.*

As much as God longs for us to love Him in return, He only wants our love if it is freely given, because, if it is not willingly offered, it is not love. I've heard those words many times before from different sources, and I thought I knew what they meant, but it is only just now, after the Father showing me a glimpse of His heart, that I can begin to understand just how important our freedom to choose is to Him. He will never violate our free will. He cannot. Love does not and cannot force relationship. It seeks, it invites, and it waits: hopefully, patiently, respectfully, and lovingly for the other to respond.

Right now, I'm thinking about what all of this means when it comes to my loving another person, the woman who will one day become my beloved. Now that I can see how the Father loves me and what that truly means, as much as I long for her life and mine to become one in the Lord, it is equally important to me that her heart freely, willingly, longingly, and unconditionally choose me.

This is the kind of love the Father desires all of us to express: the quality of love that He Himself demonstrates to us and asks us to share with each other. This is the type of love He invites each husband and wife to share in their marriage relationship, so that it can become the Heaven-on-earth oneness that God designed it to be. God wants them to experience the highest level of His goodness, glory, holiness, and love in such a beautiful, powerful, and visible way, that others who see it will want what they have, and they too will be irresistibly drawn to His heart, forever.

Give me your heart, My son, and let your eyes delight in My ways. (Proverbs 23:26 NASB)

Chapter 7: Things To Consider For Those Who Desire A Marriage Covenant Relationship

- Why exactly do you want to have a husband or wife from the Lord?
- What is your understanding of a Kingdom of God marriage relationship? How do you picture it?
- How do you think God, who designed marriage, sees it? What purpose do you think He has in establishing a marriage covenant relationship?
- Have you seen any marriages which inspire you? What elements do you recognize in them that you also want in your own marriage and feel are important?
- In what ways do you see that God has been preparing you and your heart for a marriage covenant relationship? In what ways do you think He still needs to prepare you?
- What are the qualities God has developed in you that you think your husband or wife will most be drawn to and appreciate? Do you have any qualities which you think could present difficulties or challenges for your husband or wife? What are these?
- What are the most important personal qualities you desire your husband or wife to have? Put these in order of importance to you.
- How much emotional, spiritual, intellectual, and physical room is there in your life right now for a husband or wife? Would it be enough to accomodate them? What steps would you need to take to make room for him/her?
- How much of yourself are you prepared to invest in this lifelong adventure of marriage? Are there any parts of yourself that you feel would be difficult or problematic for you to share or commit? What do you think could be blocking you from making a full commitment?
- Are there any areas of your life right now which are not fully yielded to the Lord? Do you struggle with any addictions? Did you in the past? What were those, and how did God free you from them? How do you think those areas could affect your future marriage?
- How do you see the roles within a marriage? What about decision making? Where does your framework for marriage roles come from?

- Do you want to have your own children? How many? How do you feel about adopting children? How do you envision sharing the responsibility of caring for, educating, raising, and supporting your children? What are your beliefs about family planning and birth control?
- How responsibly do you manage your money and finances? What does money represent to you? Are you more of a saver or a spender? How much of a giver are you? Do you tithe? Do you have any debts? Do you have any savings or investments? How much access does God have to your finances?
- Have you had or do you currently have any health-related concerns or issues? Have you received healing from the Lord for those? How might those issues affect your future marriage?
- Have you placed any limitations on what God could do in you and in your future marriage relationship? If so, what and why?
- Has the Lord given you or both of you a vision for your future marriage? If yes, what is it? If no, are you seeking Him about this?
- How important are creature comforts to you? What things do you really need in your everyday life to be content? Are there any things that really aren't that important to you? What? Do you have any prized possessions? Identify those and how essential they are to you.
- What are the things you most deeply desire to give to your husband or wife? What are the things you most deeply desire to receive from him or her?
- In what ways do you think you will be able to add value to your husband or wife, their growth in the Lord, and their personal development?
- In what ways do you want your husband or wife to add value to your life, your growth in the Lord, and your personal development?
- Prioritize the following: faith, family, and career. In what order of priority does your future husband or wife see these? How well would those two sets of priorities fit together?
- What kind of a home do you want to create together: physically, atmospherically, spiritually and aesthetically? How do you picture the division of labor in your home? What about pets? What kinds? Inside or outside the house?
- How do you envision the courtship/engagement process? Do you see it being a longer, or rather a shorter one? How long or short?
- What kind of wedding ceremony do you want to have (size, cost, guests, location, and level of formality)? Would your family respect what you want, or would they try to persuade you to plan it their way?
- What are the things which for you are non-negotiable: the areas of life in which you will never compromise?
- How do you imagine your relationship with your future in-laws? How would you handle areas of conflict with your own family or with your future husband or wife's family? Can you imagine any situations in which you would take the side of your own family over that of your husband or wife?

- How do you feel about and what do you need with regard to physical touch and sexual intimacy within the marriage relationship? What expectations do you have about this?
- What are your five love languages, in order of importance? What do you need to receive and experience in order to feel loved? What are your future spouse's five love languages, in order of importance? What do they need to receive and experience in order to feel loved?
- How do you envision you and your future husband or wife walking together spiritually in the Lord? What would you want or need to do, separately and together, on a daily or regular basis, in order for this to be strengthened, nourished, and kept a priority?
- How much togetherness do you want and need in your future marriage on a daily basis? How much time alone or with others?
- How easy will it be for you to share deeply personal things with your future wife or husband? Are there any areas which you would feel uncomfortable or insecure discussing with him or her? What are those? What would help you to be more open, transparent, and trusting in your communication with your spouse?
- Are there any things in your past which you would be unwilling to share with your future husband or wife? What are those, and why would you want to keep those a secret? How do you think this might affect your marriage relationship and level of trust with each other?
- What friendships are important to you which you want to continue after you are married? How do you think those would fit into your new life as a married couple? How does your future spouse feel about those friends and your relationship with them?
- How do you handle disagreement and conflict? How do you want to approach these in your marriage?
- What other issues do you think you would need to discuss and come to an understanding about with your future husband or wife before moving closer to a marriage commitment? Do you have any fears, reservations, or uncertainties about marriage in general or about your future marriage relationship? What are those? Have you had the opportunity to discuss, work on, and process those?

Chapter 8: Value

The value of something determines its price, if indeed it has one. There are some things which are of such great value, that, for the one who possesses such a treasure, the concept of price is rendered meaningless—irrelevant. The worth of that possession is so high, it simply cannot even begin to be estimated, calculated, or expressed. One neither could, nor would ever dream of attaching a price to it, let alone consider selling it, because, to them, that thing is priceless.

Because it's priceless, it's irreplaceable. There is nothing in all of the world or even beyond that could possibly take its place if it were lost, stolen, or destroyed. That thing is of inestimable value. Do you have anything like that? Is there anything in your life that has that kind of value—anything that is priceless, irreplaceable, and of inestimable value?

Out there, in the marketplace, nearly everything that has been produced or created by human hands can be assessed, assigned a monetary value, and bought or sold, if the owner is willing to part with it. When something has significant worth, it is usually insured to protect against the loss of its market value, in case it is lost, stolen, damaged, or destroyed. That insurance can cover the monetary worth, but it can't replace something that is one-of-a-kind; it can't. The best it can do is to guarantee the owner the funds necessary to substitute it with something else. That replacement may serve to take the place of that which has been lost, but, in reality, it cannot. The essence of the thing which had been present in that person's life is gone.

Now let's change the focus from something to *someone* of value. We cannot truly appreciate the value of someone unless we can also see what our life would be like without them. What would be missing or absent if that person were not there? How would our life be less meaningful and blessed without them? How would our life change without them? How would we feel in our heart without them? Would we be able to continue on without them? Would we even want to?

When we are able to recognize and appreciate the importance of someone to us, we will do all that we can to protect them. We want them to live, grow, develop, succeed, and flourish. We will look for ways to enhance, encourage, nourish, bless, honor, inspire, and embrace them. Along with these, we will give attention to them, listen to them, make time for them, try to understand them, and most importantly—love them.

In our desire and efforts to love them, we will also acknowledge and protect the freedom of that person to be who they are and to express all that is within them. We will invite them to share with us what they see and honor, without criticizing or making judgments and assumptions. If we truly love them, we will create and protect that space between us: a sacred and holy place, where both of us can approach each other with love, respect, appreciation, honesty, transparency, humility, vulnerability, joy, delight, wonder, expectation, and trust. When both of us dare to invite the Designer and Creator of all that exists to be at the center of that sacred, holy space, miracles will happen: the miraculous will become the ordinary, rather than the extraordinary.

This is the heart of the Father for marriage. This is His how He imagined, designed, and established it. This is His dream for us: to experience marriage in all of its wonder, mystery, beauty, fullness, and glory. Only a marriage like this will be able to reflect something of the wonder, mystery, beauty, fullness, and glory of who He is.

Do you want that? Have you ever dared to imagine or dream that? Have you ever asked yourself, *"Is that even possible? Could that ever exist? How could that even begin to be possible? How could any two people ever begin to imagine, let alone create and live in, a relationship like that?"*

If you have asked yourself this, you're not alone. There are probably many more of us out there who have, at some point in our life, wondered, *"what it would be like if—,"* than we know. Yet, what happened inside of us when we stopped imagining, wondering, and dreaming about that kind of marriage relationship? Why did we abandon that dream? Where did that go?

You have to be very careful who you talk to about these kinds of things: the powerful seeds of dreams that you carry deep within your heart. You can't, and you mustn't share these with just anyone. You really mustn't, because there are far too many dream-busters out there. These are people who, the second you begin to share your dream with them, will begin to give you a thousand and one reasons why that would never work—why it's just a crazy idea—why you could never ever do that—why it's just a fantasy—why you should grow up and step into the real world of their reality—and why this—and why that—and pretty soon you begin to feel very discouraged, and you wonder if it was or is really just a dream; something found in a romance novel but not in real life.

Please don't get me wrong; I'm not judging or condemning those people who try to deflate our dream balloons. They're well-intentioned, most of them. They're just talking to us from what's in their heads about life: how they've experienced it; what they've found or haven't; what they've tried to create but couldn't, and so on. They're just speaking out of a place of the limitations they have experienced and are still living in. To be honest, many of them probably think they're doing you a huge favor.

They will tell you they don't want you to get hurt or be taken advantage of by someone who will pretend to love you—someone who will then take everything from you, break your heart, and then abandon you, only to go and do the same thing to someone else. Sadly, there are far too many people out there who have experienced this kind of heartbreak at the hands of someone who had no idea of the true value of the person they were touching. That pretender failed to appreciate the dreams hidden deep within that other person.

When you were a child or a teen, it was easier to dream big dreams. Then, as you grew up, the issues and daily realities of life started to challenge those dreams. Little by little, that beautiful creative space within you that God assigned as your *dream room* began to shrink, and it became smaller and smaller— maybe it even disappeared. Perhaps your life has been so full of disappointments, failures, unfulfilled dreams, and losses, that you've just decided that all you can do now is try to survive and somehow get through the rest of your life as best you can. That's an extremely tough place to be in.

God doesn't want us to stay in a place of discouragement or despair. He's got something far better than that for each of us. He is the God of hope: the God of new possibilities, new opportunities, new dreams, new appointments, and new beginnings. He is the One who alone can make all things new. I've seen Him resurrect seemingly dead lives, relationships, marriages, and withered or dying faith. I've seen Him do it, time and time again. All He's asking of us is to dare to open up that closed part of our heart: the beautiful dream room that He created and placed deep within us. He's inviting us to give Him permission to enter there and look around with us. Then, He's asking us to give Him all of the broken pieces of our life; to just place all of those jagged fragments into His strong, kind, warm, gentle, loving, and protective Hands and just say to Him: *"I have no idea what to do with all of this mess. I've been trying for so long, but so many things have happened and now—now I don't know what to do any longer, and I can't see a way forward."*

If you'll just give Him all of those pieces, place them into His Hands, and listen, you will hear Him say to you: *"I've got this. I've got all of these broken shards, and I've got you. If you'll trust Me and allow Me, I'm going to create out of these shattered fragments a marvelous, majestic masterpiece! I am the Master of restoration. Nothing is ever lost in Me."*

I have come, that you might have life, and have it more abundantly. (John 10:10 NASB)

God is the Master Dream Builder. He placed incredible dreams in each of our hearts when we were born. He has been doing everything He can, within the framework of our free will and the effects of sin and rebellion in this world system, to help us see, feel, identify, and believe for all that He has placed within us, for His greater purposes and glory. God never gives up on our dreams, the ones He has given us. He never does, but we do sometimes.

God wants to resurrect those dreams, and, if for some reason those old dreams have expired, He desires to give us new ones! Maybe you feel like you don't really have the faith, the courage, the energy, or even the desire for a new dream, and that's okay; it really is. All you need to have is the *willingness* to allow Him to show you what that new dream is, and to trust Him to help walk you through what you need to do in order to create it. This is not rocket science; it's simple. All God is asking us to do is to just grab a hold of Him and go for it.

We often take something that is, in its essence, very simple and make it more complicated. We human beings are experts at this. We think we can improve on the simplicity of a basic truth, so we try to explain it in a much more sophisticated way. We want to sound deep and impress others, and somehow we think those extra words and explanations will bring more depth and wisdom to that understanding. If God is the one who is giving us those insights, they will bring clarity. However, if it's just man's ideas and philosophy without God, it can quickly and easily just make the simplest precept or principle so confusing that it becomes incomprehensible. When it comes to effective communication of truth and experience, less is often more, so let's strive to keep it simple.

What do you think Jesus meant when He said, *"Truly I say to you, whoever does not receive the kingdom of God like a child shall not enter it at all."* (Mark 10:15 NASB) That's a pretty radical statement! Did He really mean that? What should we take from that?

I'm a strong proponent of higher learning and of seeking wisdom, but let's be honest here. You can acquire vast bodies of knowledge and facts and even sound like you know a lot, but if you fail to see and understand the connections among all of those facts and the deeper wisdom from God which underlies them, you'll miss the whole point and have nothing to offer to the people you are teaching or training except facts—which people can get from other sources besides you—and your opinions—which are just that—your opinions. I've been in the field of education for nearly 25 years and have often been faced with the realization that, the more I learn, the more I discover there is to learn. I am a student as much as I am a teacher. There are always new lessons to be received.

We really need a serious dose of humility here. Let's stop pretending that we know it all and admit that what we understand is, in fact, only an infinitesimal part of all there is to discover. If you really want to learn something, start with the fact that, in reality, you know very little about it. If you begin there, do your homework, study His Word, ask the Lord to show you His truth, and pay close attention, He'll download concepts and revelation that will astound you and provide you with the wisdom, tools, and strategies you will need to occupy and transform spheres of influence for the advancement of His kingdom.

The fear of the Lord is the beginning of knowledge; Fools despise wisdom and instruction."
(Proverbs 1:7 NASB)
Make me know Thy ways, O Lord;
Teach me Thy paths.
Lead me in Thy truth and teach me,
For Thou art the God of my salvation;
For Thee I wait all the day. (Psalm 25:4–5 NASB)
Good and upright is the Lord;
Therefore He instructs sinners in the way.
He leads the humble in justice,
And He teaches the humble His way. (Psalm 25:8–9 NASB)

Chapter 9: Similar Hearts

If two people have been given similar hearts, it means they are on the same page. It means that things that might normally take many years to develop between them in the natural realm may only take a few days, weeks, or months, because they have already been given a very similar framework from which to see, understand, appreciate, and process everything. It also indicates they have been granted some extraordinary advantages relationally. Along with these, however, there also comes a higher level of responsibility to continually dedicate, consecrate, and commit all of this back to the Lord, so He can protect and keep it within His holy framework and boundaries.

Thus, if two people have similar hearts, it will be much easier for them:

- to share, listen, and communicate with each other
- to understand each other
- to accept and appreciate each other
- to sense where the other person is, to respect what they need at that moment, and to honor, preserve, and protect their personal boundaries
- to walk together as one
- to dream, to build, and create new things together
- to work through and solve problems, challenges, and conflicts together
- to flow together in the things of God, to sense what He wants, and to move together in that
- to minister to the Lord, to worship, and to pray together
- to minister to others
- to do life together and all that that might include
- to just be together, without needing to do or even say anything
- to experience, express, and share love to the Lord, as well as to one another and others
- to grow, develop, and mature in the things of God together
- to be open, transparent, and vulnerable to each other
- to forgive each other
- to inspire and to call out the very best of God in each other
- to honor and protect the other in all situations

- to put the other's needs before their own
- to do all they can to add value to the other in each and every situation, so that he or she will more quickly, easily, naturally, and confidently rise to their full potential in the Lord

If you desire to create, experience, and model this level of oneness with your future wife or husband, ask God to prepare your heart for His perfect choice for you—that wonderfully designed person of the opposite sex who has a heart which is very similar to yours. Although your hearts are similar, he/she won't be a carbon copy of you, so there will be more than enough differences between you to ensure that you'll both be able to learn from, complement, and balance each other for the whole length of your marriage journey together in the Lord.

Chapter 10: For Guys' Eyes Only

With a title like this, I fully expect each of you, the female readers, to come immediately to this chapter to see what's here. Absolutely! I would do the same if I saw a chapter entitled "For Feminine Eyes Only". I would! I'd be curious to see what was in that chapter and would want to discover what new insights I could receive from it. So, even though this short section is geared specifically to male readers, I hope you also will find something of interest.

What Do You See?

When you look at the woman you love, what do you see? What do you recognize in her? When you are with her, listening, talking, and sharing, are you able to perceive something unique each time you look at her? Are you able to appreciate some new aspect of who she is each occasion you spend time with her? Do you have the sense that, there is so much more to discover, that a whole lifetime wouldn't be enough?

As you are looking at her, listening to her, and thinking about her, is God awakening inside of you the desire to help draw out the very best of all that is within her? Has He shown you something of the unlimited potential He has placed within her? And, just as importantly, is He inspiring you, as a result of spending time with her, the desire to reach higher in Him—to go more deeply into the things of God and become the best man of God, for Him and with her, that you can possibly be? Have you felt anything like that?

What's going through your heart when you are with her? What kinds of emotions are you experiencing when you are together? Do you feel that your spirit is connecting with hers in some way? Do you see that her heart is connecting to yours? Can you feel that both of you have something deeper in common and are moving in the same direction?

Are these two things, your head and your heart, communicating and in agreement with each other in all of this? Are what you are thinking and what you are feeling, as you look at her and spend time with her, in harmony? Most importantly, do you have the sense that you are touching God and He is transforming you as you look at her and think about her? Has the Lord given you the sense that, in some way, as you begin to step into her world and she into yours, that you are standing on holy ground? Are you experiencing that He is also in the picture, and are you inviting Him to be?

Why am I asking all of this? It is because:

The way you see her is the way you will relate to her.

The way you see her is the way you will honor and appreciate her.

The way you see her is the way you will interact with her.

The way you see her is the way you will listen to her.

The way you see her is the way you will talk with her.

The way you see her is the way you will walk with her.

The way you see her is the way you will create with her.

The way you see her is the way you will discover with her.

The way you see her is the way you will dream with her.

The way you see her is the way you will fight for her.

The way you see her is the way you will believe with her.

The way you see her is the way you will agree with her.

The way you see her is the way you will disagree with her.

(All couples have disagreements; if you never have any, you're not communicating enough.)

The way you see her is the way you will nurture her.

The way you see her is the way you will invest in her.

The way you see her is the way you work with her.

The way you see her is the way you will work for her.

The way you see her is the way you will spend time with her.

The way you see her is the way you will touch her.

The way you see her is the way you will love her.

The way you love her is the way God will transform her into His image.

The way God is able to transform her through the quality of your love for her is the extent to which you will both experience Heaven on earth in your relationship and marriage.

So let me ask you again: what do you see?

What you see—is what there will be.

What do you want there to be?

Chapter 11: Heart Struggles

Struggles come and go. We all experience many kinds of conflicts: physical, emotional, mental, spiritual, and relational ones in our lives. Some challenges appear and just as quickly disappear, because we are given the grace to work through them quickly. Other struggles, however, are stubborn. They remain for a longer time, and though we pray about them and keep releasing them to the Lord, the issues remain. When we find ourself in this longer type of inner battle, what does God want us to do with this, and where is He in that process?

We know that He can and does work through every situation in our lives to bring good out of it: to teach us something, to give us a testimony to share with others, and to provide us with experience and wisdom, so we can be a blessing to others who are wrestling with a similar situation in their own life. *And we know that God causes all things to work together for good to those who love God, to those who are called according to His purpose.* (Romans 8:28 NASB)

We also know that every problem in life is also an opportunity, if we choose to see it as such. Yet, when we are in the problem, it is difficult and sometimes impossible to recognize that it contains within itself the miraculous potential of lifting us to a higher place of trust and intimacy with the Lord.

All struggles are, on some level, a heart issue, because the heart is at the very center of every situation of our life. When our heart is in turmoil, the conflict within us intensifies and begins to overwhelm us. No matter what the issue or problem may be, God wants our hearts to rest easy in Him. He wants us to be free of any and every thing that tries to weigh us down. He didn't design our hearts to carry heavy burdens.

Medical science has established that unresolved emotional or heart issues of any kind can create disease in our physical body through stress, grief, guilt, shame, worry, blame, resentment, bitterness, anger, and any type of toxic emotion. We all experience negative feelings, but we have to recognize, work through, and quickly release them, otherwise they will begin to manifest in our cells and create a physical problem.

Jesus said, *"Come to Me, all you who are weary and heavy laden, and I will give you rest. Take My yoke upon you, and learn from Me, for I am gentle and humble in heart; and you shall find rest* for *your souls. For My yoke is easy, and My load is light."* (Matthew 11:28–30 NASB)

Jesus has offered to carry our burdens, but there is one kind of heaviness that can seem impossible for us to let go of: self-condemnation and regret. We all make mistakes, and each time we make one, if we are quick to confess it and turn from it, God is faithful to forgive us. His heart is for us to learn from our mistake and to not make it again. He also desires for us to experience release from that burden and to walk out from it into freedom, so that nothing and no one can oppress us in any way, ever again.

Our heart and our mind both have a memory. The two organs have been designed to work together, but often they do not. Sometimes we try to delete something from our mind, but our heart cannot let go of it, or the other way around. That experience or memory remains engraved in us, and though we've experienced God's forgiveness for it, pardoning ourself eludes us. This is perhaps the hardest thing in life: to forgive ourself and let go, once and for all, of what is weighing on us.

Self is a very harsh taskmaster; it demands perfection. When we fail, which we often do, the enemy of our souls, who is constantly looking for something to use against us, immediately begins to accuse us. The accusations he tries to flood our mind with and the toxic emotions which accompany them can feel overwhelming. We can easily begin to lose hope.

The enemy is stealing, but Jesus is giving. The enemy is killing, yet Jesus is redeeming. The enemy is destroying, but Jesus is restoring. These are two opposing voices and two distinctly different outcomes. The question is, which voice will we listen to? That is really the hard part. We know that Jesus has forgiven us and is restoring us, but we still blame ourself, and we can't seem to shake that feeling of guilt and regret, no matter how hard we try.

I hear God saying to you, whoever you are, and to me, right now: *Let it go; just let it go and give it to Me. No matter how you feel, keep giving it to Me. Release yourself from that whole thing. I've already forgiven you; now, it's time for you to forgive yourself.*

There is therefore now no condemnation for those who are in Christ Jesus. (Romans 8:1 NASB)

God wants our hearts to find rest in Him. He wants us to feel and experience total freedom in Him. He desires for us to keep giving everything that is pulling or weighing us down to Him and to leave it there—all of it—with Him. It's a straightforward thing but not so easy to walk out, yet, we know that He is always with us and within us, and He will carry us through. That's who He is: loving, faithful, gentle, kind, constant, compassionate, tender, merciful, understanding, gracious, forgiving, and good. Just give your struggle to the Lord, and let it go. Jesus paid a very heavy price for our sins and mistakes. His sacrifice covers it all— everything—even your unforgiveness toward yourself. Receive the grace to forgive and love yourself; it is available to you this very moment.

God is working in you to resolve your heart issue—this inner struggle, whatever it may be, so that you can finally release it and be completely free of it, forever. He stands waiting to help you step out of that box and will then destroy it for you. He wants you to fully trust Him and find your freedom in Him. Let the guilt, regret, and shame go. Say yes to a new beginning. Stretch forth your hand toward His, grasp it, and never let go. With your hand in His and your heart within His, walk forward in freedom from this moment on.

God alone knows what His plans for our lives are, and we know His intentions are always good. The steps He has ordered for us, however, could be radically different from the ones we imagine, because He alone has the big picture. Only He knows how to arrange every detail in the best possible way. His plans for each of us are perfect—unimaginably so. That is what I am going with: His perfect plans, whatever they may be. He also wants us to tell Him what our heart desires and to commit all of our longings and plans to Him.

In all of this there is huge freedom in Him to just be ourself. He is inviting us to enjoy this very moment, each second of every day, as it is given to us, because we have no idea how many more we will receive before He calls us home to Himself. So, why burden ourself or others with our expectations about tomorrow, when we have no idea whether we will even have a tomorrow here on earth? The truth is that we will have an eternity of tomorrows with Him, and those are going to be so amazing and wonderful that we won't even begin to find words to describe them.

There is a very difficult lesson to learn here; perhaps it has taken all of my life until now to finally see and understand this basic truth:

The best way to live our life is to just delight ourself in God. This means focusing on Him before we focus on anyone or anything else.

This means putting Him at the center of everyone and everything in our life.

This means releasing everyone and everything in our life and giving them to God daily.

This means letting go of any and all expectations we have of anyone or anything and placing all of our expectations in the Lord. He is the only One we can expect from, because He is perfect, and His promises are unfailing. Everything and everyone else in our life is simply an additional gift to be received with humility and gratitude—to be treasured and handled reverently, because it is from God.

This means trusting the Lord in every situation and going forth in total confidence that He is in control.

This means refusing to carry any unnecessary baggage from our past or our present. God wants us to travel lightly.

This means embracing this very moment as His perfect gift to us and choosing to live fully, joyfully, and passionately in it.

This means experiencing the abundant life that He has promised us in *John 10:10.* This is Jesus' recipe for life. It is this way of living that I choose from this moment on, and it changes everything.

Most aspects of our lives are temporary and transient: people enter—people leave; things appear— things disappear. Doors open—doors close. Experiences begin—experiences end. God enters our life when we invite Him in, but He never forsakes or leaves us. He is always present with us, in us, and for us. What else do we really need? God has got it all; He is all.

I've always been trying to find my fulfillment at some level in other people. I knew that was never going to work, but I kept trying it anyway. I don't want that anymore; I really don't. If God brings people into my life who desire to walk with me, and I see that He is in it, I will joyfully walk with them. If God brings other people into my life who choose not to accompany me, even if I thought He wanted them to, I will ask Him to bless them and to help both of us seek Him. God is responsible for our journeys of faith, and He will accomplish His purposes in each of as we continue to move forward with Him.

Why am I stressing about people and dreams that only the Lord knows all about? That's a crazy way to live. I want to live this life passionately—without abandon. I want to just go for it—for everything that God has purposed for me. He has placed something great of Himself inside of me, and I am only just scratching the very surface of that. He deposited those things so I could honor and glorify Him, bless others, and show them how good He is so they, too, will want to know and follow Him.

God has also placed something great of Himself in you. Allow Him to show you just what that is: it's amazing and beautiful! You will have to decide, with His guidance and direction, what to do with that, who to share it with, and how to express it. Dare to explore with God what He wants you to do with all that He has placed within you. It's the stuff that dreams are made of. God created you to dream big, so do it: **dream big,** whatever it is. He is the God of big dreams; He doesn't give us small dreams. He loves the big dreams, because that's who He is: big. God is beautifully, wonderfully, majestically, and gloriously big!

I want as much of God's glorious, transforming presence in my life as I can receive. I also long to share this life with an adventurous woman of great faith who desires that too: all of God—no halfway stuff—the whole package. I desire to invest all, embrace all, risk all, and live all. That's the dream He's placed in me. It's always been there, and now it's finally time to bring it out into the real world, where the dreams God has hidden within us can become reality, if we dare to believe Him, partner with Him, and go all out. I've decided I don't want to depart this life with any of the remarkable aspects of Himself He has placed within me left unexpressed.

If others don't understand me, I'm okay with that, because He understands me, and that's enough. I'm determined to invite God to help me faithfully, creatively, and passionately live out all that He desires to entrust to me, because that is the place where He really shows up and miracles occur. I want to see the miraculous happening all around me. I desire to see the Lord manifest in every situation of life. I long to see Him touch, deliver, save, heal, restore, bless, and transform everyone around me. If they aren't receptive, I'll be asking Him to open their hearts, so they can receive everything He desires to give them.

If I sound a little crazy about all of this, I am; I confess that I am. I don't want normal; I don't want the normal package of anything. He didn't create us to be normal; He created us to be like Him. And He is not normal; He is *super*, in every category! God is far far above everything we could ever think or imagine.

"For My thoughts are not your thoughts,
Neither are your ways My ways," declares the Lord.
"For as the heavens are higher than the earth,
So are My ways higher than your ways,
And My thoughts than your thoughts." (Isaiah 55:8–9 NASB)

You are His beloved daughter or son, created in His own image. I'm His beloved son, created in His image. He created you to be like Him: He didn't create you to be normal, but extraordinary! Will you rise to the challenge? Will you dare to dream big with God?

My prayer for you is to spend more quality time with God. Allow Him to review with you where you have been and where you are now. Take inventory with Him, and ask Him to show you the next steps of His incomparable dream for your life. Finally, dare to march out boldly, in great faith, toward the amazing prophetic destiny He has purposed for you, in Jesus' mighty name! Amen!

43

Chapter 12: Heart Safari

And you shall love the Lord your God with all your heart and with all your soul and with all your might. (Deuteronomy 6:5 NASB)

….. but you shall love your neighbour as yourself; I am the Lord. (Leviticus 19:18 NASB)

These two commandments are all we really need to conduct our lives. They contain everything which is essential about how to live. These directives seem straightforward, just as many things in our human experience do, but are, in fact, challenging to walk out on a daily basis.

We know that God has instructed us to love Him fully and to love our neighbor as ourself, but what was He talking about when He commanded us to love ourself? What is that all about? We are called to serve God and others out of a heart of love and compassion. This is our basic mission in life. It applies no matter where we are, whom we are serving, or what we are engaged in, and it never changes. Yet, as we serve, we also need to discover how to love ourself, but is this selfish? There is a self-centered way of life where we always put ourself first, but I don't think that's what God is referring to here.

I believe He's saying, *"Along with your serving, I want you to embrace and cultivate a relationship with yourself: to know, love, value, invest in, listen to, communicate with, and understand yourself, in the same way you do these things in your relationships with other people. To the extent you do this, you will possess more to give and share with others and with Me."*

The problem is that many of us don't really see the importance of doing that, either because we don't understand it, or because we simply don't have time for it. In many parts of the world today, people spend their lives hurrying from one activity to the next. It's life in the fast lane: quicker, more efficient, and more productive. There's a place for all of that, there really is, but not at all costs—not even in ministry. We can rush through the days of our life doing great things for God and others, experiencing His presence and goodness, growing in faith, and trusting Him. Yet, we can still miss the deeper things that He placed in our hearts, because we never took the time or dared to go and explore there. Perhaps we were afraid if we did, we wouldn't be able to figure out what to do with what we might find, so it would just be best to leave it alone. Let God sort it out and give us whatever He wants for our lives.

God does help us sort through things, and He gives us much of what we ask for and all that we really require. He knows our needs better than we do, but there is one thing about which He waits to hear from us. I believe He wants us to express to Him what we long for—what we really want in the depth of our heart. He'll give us what we desire in the best way possible if it's right for us and we are ready for it, but first He invites us to go through the process of discovering what is hidden deep inside of us. If we miss His invitation to explore together with Him what's really in our heart, we'll miss the very best of everything He desires us to have and experience in this next season of our life. Just remember: *the really good stuff is never to be found at the surface.* The things on the surface often look attractive but have no staying power; they simply won't last. **Go for the deeper things, the hidden treasure.** You need to know, however, that finding that treasure will require some searching, digging, and a lot of processing.

God is inviting you to go on a treasure hunt, a heart safari, with Him. Before you head off on that journey, though, make sure you take the essentials with you.

Bring your compact shovel. Bring lots of water. Bring a safari hat. Bring your Bible. Bring lots of notebooks and pens. Bring some good trekking boots. Bring your sunglasses and sunscreen. Bring a sharp knife and some sturdy rope. Bring a compass. Bring a first-aid kit. Bring a sleeping bag, and a tent if you need one. Bring some matches or a lighter. Bring a flashlight. Bring some food, but don't overpack. Bring a trail cup. Bring a light pot or pan to cook with, even if you don't cook. You can even bring your smartphone, but just for letting others know you're safe and sound. Bring a map if you feel you need one, but let Him be your trail guide. He'll give you what you need each day of the journey; *He's your Daily Bread.*

Bring your imagination, as well as your curiosity. Bring your questions, along with your answers. Bring your successes and your failures. Bring your childhood, as well as your adolescence. Bring your school years and your work years. Bring your early adulthoood, as well as your later years. Bring your past relationships and your present ones, too. Bring your family and your friends. Bring your years of service and ministry. Bring your faith, as well as your doubts. Bring your struggles, along with your periods of ease. Bring your dreams, as well as your disappointments and shattered pieces. Bring your best years, along with the years when your life was a complete mess. Bring everyone and everything you've ever experienced. Don't leave anything or anyone behind. They're all on this journey with you.

Then, when you get to the end of this treasure hunt–heart safari with Him, He'll look at you, smile, give you a huge hug, and say, *"Now, you take it from here. Remember, I'll be with you on this next journey, every step of the way, and on each safari after that!"*

I will never desert you, nor will I ever forsake you. (Hebrews 13:5 NASB)

"You know where to find Me. I'm always right beside you. Go forth in full confidence, in My love. You have everything you need now. We'll meet again soon!"

Chapter 13: Heart School

"True wisdom comes to each of us when we realize how little we understand about life, ourselves, and the world around us." – Socrates[1]

There have been days when I've felt as if I have the best job in the whole world. One such day was in early October 2018, when I had a double period with a freshman intensive English class made up of two sections of 14 students each. Some days I kept both groups together, but I often split them in half, in which case one received a written task and the other had a speaking activity or discussion with me.

That day, we didn't have a classroom available, because there were language exams taking place in the room we would usually be in, and it was cold outside. One group was downstairs in the library, doing a writing assignment, while the other section was with me in the upstairs library space, which is not a classroom, but a small sitting area with twelve comfortable, red chairs placed around a low table. That area is ideal for small group discussions, because we can all see each other, and it's much less formal than a normal classroom situation. It is easier there for students to relax, open up, and share their ideas with each other.

I had planned something else for that first period, but, as we had no laptop or smart board, it turned out to be a discussion about a wide variety of everyday topics and a chance for me to get to know the students better. Those young people showed themselves to be delightfully open, intelligent, flexible, and creative, so I felt certain it was going to be an excellent school year with them. During the second period, we had our regular classroom, so I showed both groups two videos about Kyle Maynard. The first chronicled his climbing Mount Kilimanjaro, and the second featured an interview of Kyle with Oprah Winfrey. After Nick Vujicic, Kyle is the next inspirational speaker I have my groups listen to, and, when he speaks, students are always fully attentive. As I was looking around the room at the group while we were watching Kyle that day, the Lord gave me three words: *"Potential! Possibility! Perfection!"*

I immediately wrote those down, and, during the next break, as I sat with those words, He added, ***"See their potential, show them the possibilities, and inspire them to perfection!"*** I realized in that moment that this is what the vocation of teaching is really all about.

I've always believed this was important and have tried to practice it, but this was the first time those three words and expressions came into focus together. It was a teachable moment and one I will never forget.

A few weeks after that, during a demonstration English period held on an open house day at the same school here in southern Hungary, that same advanced level freshman English group and I were sitting around a semi-circle at the front of the classroom. We were discussing a film based on a true story we had just finished watching, with close to 90 guest students and parents present to observe and listen to our discussion.

Each of the thirteen students present had chosen a particular focus question about the film and was asked to share their thoughts about that. The students prepared very well, and the discussion was going smoothly. One student, who had decided to critique the film we had watched, shared that that film has everything in it, because it covers everything important about life: family, relationships, school, work, life purpose, love, challenges, decisions, and destiny. Another student spoke about the meaning of the title of the film, *"Unconditional;"* that it refers to unconditional love—the way that God loves us and wants us to love others and ourself. She added that many people think that love can quickly run out, so they are very careful about whom they love and how much they love them, because they are afraid they might not have enough. She went on to say that love works in just the opposite way: that if we choose to love others unconditionally, we'll find that love, which starts as a stream, will slowly turn into a river, and the river will then flow in a sea, or an ocean—endless—limitless.

At that point, I picked up a sheet of paper and started taking notes, because I wanted to remember what was being said. *Life tip: Always have a piece of paper and a pen on you, because you never know when you're going to hear something really important, and when you do, write it down immediately, so you won't forget it.* Toward the end of that open house day demonstration English class, the Holy Spirit gave me some great follow-up questions to ask the group, and from that point on, our discussion really began to take off.

I asked them, *So, during our school years we have subjects we learn, study, and take tests on. We know what those subjects are, but in the school of life that we are in, what are those life-school subjects that we are learning?* Several students offered their thoughts about that, and we ended up with a pretty good list. Then I asked the group, *So, which subjects are more difficult for you: school subjects or life-school subjects?* All of them responded, *"life-school subjects."* I asked them why that was, and they explained why they felt that way, with several of them giving specific examples.

Then, one of the students mentioned that, in our life-school, every person and situation we meet can be our teacher, if we recognize them as such. I stopped for a moment to let that sink in, and I quietly asked myself; *How is it possible that this young person knows this essential truth about life at the age of fourteen when it took me many years beyond that age to see that?*

I followed up with this question, *So, who are your life-school teachers?* They came up with an amazing list again, and the same student who had shared with us that each person and situation in our life can be our teacher said, *"We ourself can also be one of our teachers; we can learn from our own mistakes and not make that same mistake again."* I paused briefly to allow that thought to settle, then I asked everyone, Have you ever learned something from someone else's mistakes or from their negative example? All of them raised their hand, and a few of the students shared a brief example of that. The bell was just about to ring, so I thanked the students for their participation and our guests for joining us.

That class period was one of the most beautiful and powerful conversations I have ever had with a group of students. Over the years, I have been privileged to have a number of quality discussions like that with groups of young people at Horváth Mihály Gimnázium, Szentes, Táncsics Mihály Gimnázium, Orosháza, Batsányi János Gimnázium,

Csongrád and Deák Ferenc Gimnázium, Szeged. In fact, during the 2018-19 school year, the best group I have ever worked with in 25 years of teaching, a class of Horváth Mihály Gimnázium seniors specialized in English, continued to amaze me every time I met them by the incredible wisdom, sensitivity, compassion, intelligence, creativity, humor, and spontaneity with which God has so richly blessed each of them.

This group of seniors is what I would call, *my dream class.* I told them, at the end of last school year, as I looked around the circle at each of their faces: *I only recognize a tiny little bit of what God has placed inside each one of you, and there's a whole lot more within you than I can see. You have right now, within you, both individually and collectively, everything that is necessary to change the world. You could change your country, any country in Europe, or any country in the world with what you carry inside of you—you really can. I thank God for the awesome privilege of being one of your teachers these past three years.*

How often does a teacher have the chance to say something like that to a group of their students? This might sound strange, but this thought has just come to me at this moment: if my life has had no other purpose than to try to speak words of life, truth, and encouragement into these young people's lives and destinies, that in itself would be more than enough, it really would.

When we're born into this world, we are automatically enrolled in life-school. Some of us get a very good start and are blessed to have a family who love and protect us, provide us with the basic necessities, and do all they can to ensure that we grow up in a safe and healthy environment.

Many other children around the world, however, are not so fortunate. Some of them have literally nothing, and every day they struggle against great odds just to survive. We must do all that we can to help change that situation, so that every child, in each part of the world, has the opportunity to not only survive, but to grow up in a secure, nurturing environment—so that they, too, can experience the good future and a hope that our Heavenly Father desires for them.

This is a mission that each and every one of us needs to embrace, in whatever ways we can, to make a difference. It doesn't take much to have a positive impact on another person's life. All you have to do is give what you have. Just release it, dedicate it to the Lord, ask Him to bless and multiply it, and then watch it grow. Go back and read *Matthew 14:14–21*, where more than five thousand people were fed from two loaves of bread and five fishes. It doesn't take much to feed five thousand, let alone one child, when we simply give whatever we have. We offer what we have, God shows up, and that small amount of something suddenly becomes more than enough. We need to make sure, however, that what we are offering someone is really what is needed and what is best for them.

All children deserve the chance to get a good education that will prepare and equip them for a successful life. Having competent, caring teachers is a vital part of that process. Teaching is not just a job; it is a vocation, one of the most important ones in the world, because teachers can influence a student's way of thinking and entire future. Every educator bears an enormous responsiblity to the students they teach, their parents, and ultimately to God, for the role they play in the nurturing and development of the young lives they help shape.

In November 2019, the interviewers and sound crew of a Hungarian national radio station came from Budapest to Szentes to do a feature program about Horváth Mihály Gimnázium, one of the two schools where I have been teaching.

The radio interview team spoke with our Principal and several teachers, as well as with several students, to try to get an accurate picture of what kind of learning/teaching community and environment the school provides. I was privileged to be one of the teachers they interviewed, and the day before that, I asked my dream class, the advanced group of the 12As, if they would be willing to help me prepare by doing a mock interview with me in Hungarian, so I would be able to answer whatever questions which might be asked me in an intelligent, expressive, and grammatically correct manner.

Of course, my dream class said, yes, they would, and we spent that hour practicing. I asked each of them to come up with at least one really pertinent question about education, learning, teaching, and my work and years as a teacher here in Hungary, which they did. I also asked one of the students to make note of any mistakes I made, along with corrections, as well as any important or relevant expressions which might be useful in the interview.

During that mock interview, which was a lot of fun for me and for the students, when there was a finer point of grammar that I didn't really understand, they tried to explain to me what the rule was or why it worked that way. Most of the time, they managed to do that quite successfully, but there were a few instances where I could see that, even for them, some of our top students, there were some aspects of their own native language which remained elusive in terms of what something meant or how it was used. Nevertheless, they still managed in each case to come up an explanation or clarification. That hour was a kind of revelation for me, and I felt: *This is what school should really be all about! Everyone is teaching and everyone is learning! I love this! This is exactly what I had hoped my future teaching would be like when I was in graduate school preparing to become a teacher!*

We are greatly blessed if God has given us wonderful school and life-school teachers. Each of us is a product of all those people who have spoken into our lives in some way—either positively or negatively. We are all given the awesome privilege and huge responsibility of speaking positive words into the lives and destinies of those people around us with whom we have influence. In a very real sense, we are all, at the same time, both heart-school and life-school teachers and students.

Let's determine today to become the best possible heart-school students and teachers God desires us to be. Let's also invite Him into the center of our life-school and allow Him to choose our curriculum, design our courses, plan our lessons, present the material to us, and give us tests on what we have learned. Then, with great faith, commitment, love, determination, and industriousness on our part, there will come the wonderful day when He will graduate us and allow us to enroll in even more advanced level courses—for His glory, our edification, and for blessing others. Amen!

My son, do not forget my teaching,
But let your heart keep my commandments;
For length of days and years of life,
And peace they will add to you. Do not let kindness and truth leave you;
Bind them around your neck,
Write them on the tablet of your heart.
So you will find favor and good repute
In the sight of God and man. (Proverbs 3:1–4 NASB)

Chapter 14: The Christmas Heart

The Advent season and Christmas are a time for us to focus on the miracle of the birth of Jesus, who came to earth just over two thousand years ago. His birth took place several months before the date on which we celebrate Christmas. The Christmas holiday itself has its origins in pagan traditions, which means it isn't at all one of the seven Jewish feast or festival periods at which God has appointed for us to meet with Him. Nevertheless, He is Lord over all—over each day of the year; every day belongs to Him, including the day on which we celebrate His birth.

Advent is the period when we choose to focus on the mystery of His birth and why He came. It is a time of preparation of our hearts and lives to receive Him. Each day of the year can, and should be an advent. It is the only day we have—the present one—to receive, love, honor, celebrate, serve, and commune with God.

Despite its pagan origins, I love the colors, sounds, and ambience of the Christmas season. I feel a sense of excitement in having the chance to share the true meaning of this time of year with the people I know. That's why I usually write a special message which focuses on the meaning of Jesus' coming and birth and share that in English or Hungarian with those people God has brought into my life, both here in Hungary, and back home in the United States.

I especially love the beautiful Christmas carols of this season, most of all the ones which have a message about God's unconditional love for us and His coming in the form of a helpless Baby. Silent Night is my favourite. I could sing that carol each day of the year, and, in fact, many days I do, sometimes with a piano accompaniment. There's a wonderful sense of awe and beauty in the lyrics of that carol, and it often brings me to tears as I sing and play it.

When we were children growing up in Lancaster, Pennsylvania, the Christmas Eve carol services were heavenly moments for me. My siblings and I all sang in one of the choirs at First Presbyterian Church in Lancaster, and we were blessed to have one of the greatest, most dedicated ministers of music and organists, Mr. Reginald Lunt. Mr. Lunt inspired all of us who grew up under his tutelage to love and sing great music as a way of worshipping God. Our weekly choir practices never finished until he was satisfied that the sounds we were producing would be acceptable to the Lord. Perfection, or as close to that as possible, was always the goal.

That Christmas Eve carol service was the stuff that legends are made of. Though I no longer live there in Lancaster, on Christmas Eve, at least a part of my heart is always there, in the beautiful sanctuary of that church building, with its gorgeous, ethereal, stained-glass windows warming the entire space with their soft glow, as everyone holds a candle and sings Silent Night. That part of the service remains indelibly engraved within my heart as one of the most beautiful moments of worship and community that I have ever experienced, and I long to experience that again.

I think God wants us to develop and live our lives out of *a Christmas heart*. What is a Christmas heart? First of all, it is one which is centered in the Lord—in His extravagant love, beauty, graciousness, mercy, lovingkindness, righteousness, holiness, and tender care for us. It is a heart which longs for a deeper and more intimate relationship and walk with Him. It is a heart which dares to respond to all that He has done for us, with such abandonment, that we say to Him, *"What I desire is to live in Your presence and to be Your light to a broken, lost, and dying world."*

The world around us desperately needs more light. There's a lot of darkness all around us, but when we stand up boldly and display the radiance that He has placed within us, that darkness is dispelled. The environments we have influence over then begin to brighten, become more alive, and resound with joy, because God is present—offering hope and restoration to all who will receive Him.

This is the true message of the Christmas season: that the light, love, and mercy of God have come down to us in human form to save and restore us, and that, out of love, Jesus lay down His own life so that we might live forever with Him. All we have to do is say yes to what He has done for us and then follow Him.

Many years ago, shortly after I had arrived here in Szentes, one of my closest friends and his family invited me for lunch to their place in a small town about an hour from here, on the third day of Christmas. Not long after we had finished eating, the doorbell rang, and there stood a man who had come to deliver the tragic news that the younger sister of my friend's mother had just been killed in a car accident earlier that morning. The sense of grief in that apartment was overwhelming. My friend, his girlfriend, and I decided to go outside for a long walk to allow the mother, father, and older sister some time alone to grieve and mourn. We stayed out there most of the afternoon.

When we came back inside several hours later, my friend's mother and her older sister were both sitting there on the couch in the living room, knitting a sweater. The material was one of the most beautiful I had ever seen. My friend asked his mother what they were doing, and she replied, *"Tim, you came here today wearing a very thin sweater and an autumn, not a winter coat. We were worried about you not being warm enough, so we decided to knit you this sweater. It's almost finished, so you'll be able to wear it home with you today."*

When I heard those words and realized what they had done for me, I was touched to the very core of my being. How could those two precious sisters, having just lost their beloved younger sister in a car accident and surely grieving in the depths of their hearts, have the capacity to express such a generous act of kindness toward someone who wasn't even a family member? At a time of such deep personal loss, they had chosen to focus on doing something good for someone else and blessing them through the creative work of their own hands. As I thanked and hugged both of them, I sensed the presence of God in such a beautiful and unforgettable way, and I shall never forget the exceptional generosity of their hearts toward me that Christmas.

In early December 2010, one of my mother's closest friends emailed me from the States to let me know that my mother was nearing the end of her earthly journey, and, that if I wanted to see again before she passed on, I would need to fly home as soon as possible. When I went online to book a flight, all of the airlines I usually travel with were already fully reserved for the dates I wanted. There were no economy class seats available, not even one. I kept searching and finally found one seat on U.S. Airways from Budapest to Zurich, and then on to Philadelphia. I had never flown U.S.

Airways to or from Europe before that—usually British Airways, Lufthansa, KLM, or Air France, but those airlines had no seats. I booked my flights and let my family know I would be arriving there a few days before Christmas.

What I didn't know when I bought my tickets was that a huge winter storm would several weeks later hit most of Western and much of Eastern Europe, and that all of the major airports in Western Europe would be shut down for several days, right at the time I would be flying back to the States. God knew, however, He was in the details, and He arranged everything perfectly. My younger sister saw the weather reports coming from Europe. She emailed my siblings to let them know there was little or no chance I would be able to fly out because of the severe winter storms, and to not expect me for Christmas.

There were only two airports open which continued to handle incoming and outgoing flights right when I was departing: Budapest and Zurich. To this day, I just marvel and give thanks that God prearranged every detail of that trip home to make sure I would have those two weeks during the Christmas season with my mother, just before she went home to be with the Lord.

When I arrived in Philadelphia, my mother's best friend's husband was there to meet me and drive me back to their home in Lancaster. They kindly let me stay with them, lent me one of their cars so I could drive back and forth to the hospice where my mother was being cared for, and made sure I had everything I might need. I am eternally grateful to them for their generosity and support, which made it possible for me to spend as much of that time there with my mother, my siblings, and their families.

That two-week period was the most beautiful, precious, and memorable Christmas of my entire life. I could see that my mother was in the last days of her earthly journey. It was very difficult for her to communicate with me, but we did enjoy some short periods of conversation and prayer together. I cried many tears there with her: tears of appreciation for all that she had meant to me, given to me, and taught me over the years; tears of thanksgiving for all the wonderful times of shared visits and travels together, and tears of gratitude to God for giving me and my siblings the most amazing mother and role model of faith, courage, hope, love, and kindness that one could ever hope for.

Looking back again now on that Christmas, my heart is filled with thanks to God for giving me the gift of those days together with my mother. I shall always treasure that time with her and my siblings. I encourage you to be thankful for the times you have with your own family and loved ones and to be grateful for each moment together. We have no way of knowing just when any of us might be called home to be with the Lord, so we should embrace every opportunity we have to love, bless, and be kind to our family members. May God help each of us cultivate a true *Christmas heart* which is rooted in His unshakeable love.

For God so loved the world, that He gave His only begotten Son, that whoever believes in Him should not perish, but have eternal life. For God did not send the Son into the world to judge the world; but that the world should be saved through Him. (John 3:16–17 NASB)

Chapter 15: Yellow Lanterns

Two summers ago, I bought these two beautiful, inexpensive, yellow, solar lanterns for the garden. I took them out of the boxes(so they could be out-of-the box lanterns!), hung them out in the sun all day, then brought them inside after dark, but they didn't light. I figured they hadn't gotten enough of a solar charge, so, the next day, I hung them out again—the result was the same. I brought them back inside, put them in the back pantry on a shelf, and forgot about them until this past summer. I hung them out again, but they still didn't light.

My jack-of-all-trades, mechanical genius neighbour, Aladár, whose nickname is Ali, came over to look at the lanterns with me, and found a way to take the tops off. They didn't look like they were designed to come off, but they did. Inside each lantern, there was a tiny, barely visible on/off switch, so we flipped the switch to the "on " position in each lantern and put the tops back on. I hung the lanterns out all day, and, voila: they started lighting! Did I read the instruction manual before I tried to use them? Yes, I did, and I looked for the on/off switch on the outside of the lanterns, but didn't see any, so I figured the manual was wrong (don't laugh!). I know the manual usually contains accurate information, and, next time, I will reread it to make sure I haven't missed anything important.

So, why am I telling you about these yellow solar lanterns? On the packaging boxes the lanterns came in, it was written that the maximum lighting time after a full day's charge was six hours. When I read that, I thought, *Okay, if I bring them inside at 9:00 p.m. that means they should be lighting until 3:00 a.m. That's great!* So, I brought one into my bedroom/living room, and the other I hung in the entrance hallway. I was mesmerized by the soft, yellow glow the lanterns gave off; it was beautiful!

When I woke up the next morning, about eight hours later, the lantern in my room was still lighting and so was the one in the hallway. I thought to myself, *These are really good lanterns! I got two hours more light than the manufacturer specified!* The following night, the same thing happened. The third night, I brought them inside around 6:00 p.m. At 10:00 a.m. the following morning, they were still lighting, which was sixteen hours of light. Amazing!

So, here's my question: *Was the instruction manual wrong about this, or were these solar lanterns just supernaturally anointed by God to furnish light well beyond my expectations? What do you think?* Either way, I love the light these lanterns give off. If they have them for sale again this season, I plan to buy two more of them. That way, if God at some point in the future should graciously give me the privilege of visiting my new friend in the country where she is serving the Lord, I'll be able to bring her those lanterns, so she and the community she ministers to there can enjoy them too!

Sometimes in life, we try to improvise our way through situations without bothering to first "read the instructions". We don't carefully read through the user manual written by the manufacturer before we start to use the device we have purchased. The manufacturer designed that product, and they know exactly what it is designed to do, how it should be operated, and what maintenance must be carried out at certain intervals to make sure it provides a long period of reliable service to its owner.

God has given us His Word, the Holy Bible, which is His set of instructions—His *Owner's Manual* for life. It contains everything we need to know about who He is, who we are, what He has done for us through Jesus, and how to live. His Word is full of amazing, 100%-reliable promises.

If we choose to receive, trust, and follow the One who designed and created us, and invite Him to be our guide and power source, then, we will, just like those yellow solar lanterns and their longer-than-expected lighting capacity, enjoy the wonderful extended benefits guaranteed to us—one of which is a long life.

Because He has loved me, therefore I will deliver him;
I will set him securely on high, because he has known My name.
He will call upon Me, and I will answer him;
I will be with him in trouble;
I will rescue him, and honor him,
With a long life I will satisfy him,
And let him behold My salvation. (Psalm 91:14–16 NASB)

Chapter 16: Thinking Three in the Marriage Relationship

I've heard it said that mathematics is the language of the universe. That's an interesting concept, and I believe there is a measure of truth in that. Mathematics is one of the most important languages of the universe, but it's not the primary one: *love is.*

In the heart of God, marriage is not about two; it's about three: you, your spouse, and the Lord. When the two of you take the wonderful, faith-filled step of committing your lives and destinies to each other in Him, God desires to be at the very center of your marriage relationship and daily activities. When you invite Him to be the focus of everything, everything becomes possible. Everything!

For nothing shall be impossible with God. (Luke 1:37 NASB)

God knows that two together are better than one. Two together are stronger than one. Two together are more effective than one. Two together are more resilient than one. Two together are more resourceful than one. Two together are more creative than one. Two together are more insightful than one. Two together are more dynamic than one. Two together are more strategic than one. Two together are more constructive than one. The amazing thing about two being better than one is, that when we add God to the equation, in heavenly mathematics, one plus one equals three!

According to K. Gallagher, the number three in Hebrew can signify counsel, stability, balance, new life, resurrection, strength, fruitfulness, and unity. The pictographic meaning can refer to maturing, nourishing, ripening, benefitting, and rewarding. A geometric representation of this is the three equal sides of the triangle which, when joined together, form a strong, balanced unit and foundation.[1]

When God Himself is invited into the center of a marriage, the power of two becoming one in the natural is supernaturally turbocharged with all of the infinite resources of Heaven. In that holy place, where He abides within the two people, and in the oneness He alone can create out of the space between them, all of Heaven smiles, rejoices, and begins to mobilize—and all of hell begins to tremble, because it means the Father's love is radically advancing in this world, and the powers of darkness are retreating.

We have literally no idea of the infinite, unlimited power of God's love waiting to be released when a man and a woman united in love, holy matrimony, and equal partnership, invite the Creator of the universe to be fully at the center of every detail of their daily lives. Why else do you think the enemy is focusing so much attention on trying to subvert and destroy God's design and plan for marriage in nearly every country and society in the world today?

When God graciously brings me to the place of stepping into the wonderfully unparalleled adventure of covenant marriage with the woman I will commit myself to, I am going to invest all that I am and have together with her, placing God at the center. I desire for her to feel that she is cherished and deeply loved above all other women. I want God to be fully present in our relationship, each moment of every day, to create the beautiful symphony of two hearts becoming one. The Lord is waiting for each engaged and married couple to ask Him to do what He alone can: fill the marriage relationship with His glory, so that His presence, beauty, and majesty will be seen, felt, and experienced.

God is asking permission to be Himself in the space between ourself and our beloved—a space with no distance, time, or limitation. In marriage, we step into His heavenly dimension: a place of exquisite intimacy in Him and a place we will want to remain in forever with our beloved. He can produce within and between us what we cannot create by ourselves. God can make up for what we lack; He desires to bestow on us all that we need and desire. He will manifest what we cannot establish by ourselves. He alone can restore what has been damaged, lost, destroyed, or neglected, if we'll give Him the broken pieces, ask forgiveness, and invite Him to lead us.

I wish that every person in the world could visualize this: the unlimited possibilities of God creating His heavenly dimension in every marriage so that He can birth something totally amazing and beautiful that has never been seen on this earth before: *a unique expression of His glory, beauty, and majesty!* This is His heart for marriage: to reveal a glorious aspect of who He is in a totally original and delightful way through each couple's unique, particular marriage. It won't be visible or expressed to the world at any other time in history or in any other way, except through this couple. Just stop and think about what that really means for a minute. Allow the power of that concept to soak in and settle deep within the recesses of your heart and mind.

God wants each married couple to experience something of the quality of oneness and heart intimacy that He—the Father, He—the Son, and He—the Holy Spirit enjoy and share with each other in that mystical, miraculous relationship we call the Trinity. How does that work? Again, we're stepping onto His level and can only perceive a tiny measure of the full splendor of that glorious Community. If He tried to show us more, it would be overwhelming. We wouldn't be able to receive or contain it, because the Trinity is perfect love, perfect fellowship, perfect understanding, perfect communication, perfect co-operation, perfect harmony, perfect joy, and perfect intimacy. Could that ever become possible for us in our human experience?

The answer is both yes, and no. It's no, because we aren't yet fully transformed into His likeness, so our experience will be something less than perfection, but it's also yes, because, even in our countless imperfections, He will grant us wonderful grace with periods of perfected relationship. This is the incredible vision that He showed me in Jerusalem at the 2018 Convocation: something that He engraved permanently onto the pages of my heart after He introduced me to someone He described as *the hidden treasure.* She is one of the Lord God's beloved daughters, and He revealed to me just how beautiful and cherished she is to Him. He showed me that she is priceless, irreplaceable, and of infinite worth. Since that moment, I only want to see and relate to her the same way that our Heavenly Father does. I can't find words adequate to express how profoundly this has begun to transform my life. I will never be the same again.

A man and a woman—a son and a daughter—together—in the Lord—three in one. It's an incomprehensible, unfathomable mystery: a beautiful, dazzling, powerful, and glorious reality as well. Marriage is the intersection of a divine and human encounter which is to be entered in to and lived out of with great reverence, passion, joy, expectation, abandonment, delight, sacrifice, adventure, spontaneity, and love. Why are we settling for so much less in marriage, when so much more is available? Do we have more faith in our fears, failures, and brokenness than in His promises? God is not surprised or shocked by our selfish intentions, missed opportunities, confusing communication, misplaced loyalties, divided attention, shameful betrayals, regrettable mistakes, bitter disappointments, shattered pieces, irreconcilable differences, unkept promises, enslaving addictions, and broken hearts. He is well acquainted with it all.

Some of Jesus' last Words on the Cross were: *"Father forgive them; for they do not know what they are doing."* (Luke 23:35 NASB) Without Him at the center of our lives and relationships, we have no idea what we are doing or where we are going. He's shown me that the three greatest obstacles to my deepening in Him and being in true relationship with someone else are my pride, my stubbornness, and my selfishness. There is only one remedy for these three impediments: they must be put to death—daily.

I have been crucified with Christ; and now it is no longer I who live, but Christ lives in me; and the life which I now live in the flesh I live by faith in the Son of God, who loved me, and delivered Himself up for me. (Galatians 2:20 NASB)

God all too well knows that we are going to have some crazy, confusing, very messy days between ourself and the one we love—days when we will feel like things are breaking hopelessly apart and we have no idea how to even begin to put them back together again. He's fully aware we're going to have some days when we look at the other person and wonder how in the world they could ever say or think something like that. He realizes we're going to have some days when we're just plain worn out, exhausted, beaten down, depressed, or defeated—when we'll just want to withdraw from everyone and everything. He understands we're going to have some days when we are convinced that we married the wrong person. He knows we're going to have some days when we feel unappreciated, taken for granted, misunderstood, and unloved by the person we have chosen. He also is aware that there may be days when we or the person we love will do something that so deeply wounds the other's heart, that forgiveness seems impossible.

God sees and understands all of this. He also reassures us that He is there to help us get through those days and press on through them to better ones. Through all of this, He's perfecting us and has a wonderful destiny ahead for us, if we'll just continue trusting and walking with Him and each other.

God wants us to keep going, even when the way becomes too difficult; to keep trusting, even when we feel lost and confused; to keep getting back up, even when we have nothing left; to keep praying, even when we don't receive an answer; to keep loving, even when we feel nothing inside; to keep believing, even when our faith is on empty; to keep declaring His Word and promises, even when we don't see any results; to keep saying yes, even when we'd rather say no.

The Lord is asking us to keep dreaming, building, and reaching higher in Him, no matter what comes. He will lift us up and accomplish all He has purposed to do in and through us. He is the *Master Architect*, the *Master Builder*, and the *Master Sustainer*. Just give it all to Him, and watch what He will do. He can and will do it. Everything!

Now to Him who is able to do exceeding abundantly beyond all that we ask or think, according to the power that works within us, to Him be the glory in the church and in Christ Jesus to all generations forever and ever. Amen. (Ephesians 3: 20–21 NASB)

Chapter 17: Pure in Heart

God has such astounding things planned for us that we could never even dare to imagine them. His heart is so good, so gracious, so beautiful, and so holy that we can't even stand in His presence, yet He desires to share His heart and reveal Himself to us as we step closer in intimacy with Him.

Deep down, all of us are searching for intimacy. This is our deepest desire, even if we are unaware of it. God has placed this profound inner yearning within us—a longing that we unsuccessfully try to fill with other things. We're all on a journey attempting to discover this deep sense of connectedness: this perfect place of feeling, knowing, and experiencing that we are deeply loved, that someone cherishes us, and that we can also love someone with all of our heart. This is our most basic and important human need. The Lord God placed this within us at the very beginning when He created Adam out of the dust of the earth and then fashioned Eve out of the material He created Adam out of, except He designed Eve completely differently. Thank God that He did! He also breathed His Spirit into them, and they each became a living spirit, just as He is. God deposited something of His essence into the first man and woman, because He designed mankind to be like Him. That is still His intention and purpose, that we be a reflection of Him.

We're all trying to get back there to the Garden of Eden—to the very beginning—to the place where everything was perfect and the first man and woman were walking in delightful, harmonious relationship and communion with God and each other. It was effortless, natural, and wonderful. At the core of our being, we all have the sense that this is what our lives and relationships are meant to be like, and we really hunger for this. It's such a powerful need, that it is extremely easy to mistake something or someone else for the very best that God desires for us; to try to satisfy that need with a false substitute. The world is full of seductive attractions and cheap imitations that call to us; they try to get our attention and lure us away from the real, which is God, into the unreal, which is where the enemy of our souls resides.

Sin means missing the mark. It means we're aiming at the target we want to hit, but the arrow misses it altogether. It has no chance of hitting it, because we're pointing the bow in the wrong direction. Our aim is off, imprecise, and misaligned, so our arrow strikes something else, and it may become so embedded that we can't even pull it out. That's what addiction does: it traps us in an enticement that is so far removed from the pure, satisfying love and intimacy with God and one another we long for, that those two opposite worlds become universes apart. That's how great the gulf is that separates the two.

God desires to restore us to Himself: to that unspoiled, unimaginably beautiful place of deep, satisfying relationship and love with Him. That's what He longs for, and that's why He sent His only Son, Jesus, to earth to be born, to grow up, to teach, to model, and, finally, to suffer and sacrifice His life to atone for all of our missed marks—from the very beginning—until the very end. His sacrifice covers it all, if we will come to Him, give Him everything, receive His forgiveness, surrender our lives and our wills, and allow Him to transform us into the perfect image and reflection of Himself that He long ago designed and breathed into mankind.

It's a person-by-person restoration process, and it takes a lot of time, mercy, compassion, and patience on His part. After we make the decision to accept Him and make Him the captain of our ship, it takes the rest of our life. God isn't in a hurry; we are, but He isn't. He wants to make sure it's done right. Along the way, He has important work for each of us to do: to share what He has done for us with others, to bless them, and to invite them to come along with us on the same journey back to the Father's love. He also commissions us to reclaim territory that the enemy has stolen, so that His kingdom of love, goodness, and righteousness will continually advance here on the earth.

Thy Kingdom come. Thy will be done, on earth, as it is in heaven. (Matthew 6:10 NASB)

It's a journey you don't want to miss and the only one there really is. It's the only quest that really matters, because all of the other things that we now feel are so important in life are going to be burned up, one day in the very near future, and all that will remain is what He has accomplished in us and what we have done out of love for Him. Everything else that we had thought was so important—all of the other things that we had spent so much of our time, energy, and resources focusing on, in the wrong direction—are going to disappear, forever. God wants us to construct our house on solid rock, the Rock of His Son. All other foundations are just sinking sand, and when the waves and tsunamis of life and the final judgment come crashing in, as they will, the life that is built on the foundation of sand will be gone, forever separated from Him; only the life that is established on the Rock will remain.

Sand foundations only erode, crumble, and collapse. The Lord wants our foundations to be secure. God is always searching for us, whispering to us, and inviting us to come closer and discover who He is. He is constantly calling to us: daring us to imagine, believe, receive, and create with Him the best life we could ever imagine. It's so good that most of us are reluctant to believe it. We think that it's just a fantasy, because all we can see is the real world around us, which in reality is the unreal world—the one which has been so horribly distorted and deformed by the ravages of sin and rebellion over the past six thousand years that the Creator Himself barely recognizes it. God created everything that exists to be perfect, and it was so until the first Adam and his Eve made the wrong choice: they listened to the wrong voice.

All of us have done the same: we've been listening to the wrong voice. Sometimes it's our own voice—our tiny, selfish voice —clamoring to always be in the center. Sometimes it's the enemy's voice—the seduction, deceit, and destruction that lies at the core of all he does. Sometimes it's the voices of others—pressuring us to follow the crowd and be like everyone else. Sometimes it's the voice of unmet desires in our own heart—pulling us in the wrong direction. Whichever it is, if it's not in agreement with God, it's always the wrong voice—always. We have to decide which one we're going to listen to, and that decision is one we make continuously, each moment of every day.

God is always communicating something to us, and, even when He appears to be silent, He is still conveying a message. The problem isn't on His end; it's on ours. He's always sending out signals, beckoning us to tune out the other, distracting noises in our lives and to tune in to His voice. Most of the time, we miss Him, because our attention is focused elsewhere. Do you have any idea how frustrating that might be to God? I don't know if He feels frustration, because He is perfect, but He does have emotions, and, because we were created in His image, we have them too. In the Bible, we find many instances of God expressing His emotions. The only difference is that His emotions are holy and of perfect intention. He desires to transform us so that our feelings and thoughts will become as right-intentioned as His are.

If you've ever fallen in love with someone and experienced what that is like, you have a tiny idea of how God feels about us. Now, if we multiply how you felt by a billion to the trillionth power, we might just begin to comprehend something of the intensity of God's love for us. When you fell in love with your beloved, you felt passionately about them. You wanted to hold them close to you; you longed to be with them and do everything together, and you desired to share every moment and experience with them. You just wanted to lose yourself in them and stay in that place forever. Nothing else seemed to matter except being with them.

It's the most beautiful thing in the world to be totally in love with someone and for them to be completely in love with you. Nothing even begins to compare with that. Some people spend their whole lives looking for someone with whom they can experience that, but, most of the time, even if they find that person, they will experience disappointment. At times, their love will fail the other person, the other person's love for them will fall short, and the depth of the passion they first experienced together will, in most cases, begin to fade, diminish, and sometimes even disappear. Is that how it is supposed to be?

Why would God put that intense longing inside of us for deep, satisfying love and not give us a way of experiencing that throughout our life? Is that how He operates? Would He just allow us to enjoy a tiny bit of that and then watch us struggle in our disappointment and disillusionment? Would He do that? You'll have to answer that question for yourself, but, if you know Him and are walking with Him, you already know the answer to that question: no, He wouldn't. That's simply not who He is.

His intentions toward us are only good. Jeremiah 29:11 sums it all up, *"For I know the plans that I have for you,"* *declares the Lord, "plans for welfare and not for calamity to give you a future and a hope."*(NASB)

I invite you to take a few moments now and meditate on that. What do you think that good future and a hope looks like for you? Have you experienced anything of that in your life until now? Has God shown up and begun to create that with you? If He has, right now might be a very appropriate time to make a list of the specific ways He has done that and to thank Him for those, to really thank Him. Perhaps you've forgotten the many miraculous things He has already accomplished in your life. God wants you to remember those specific occasions of His goodness toward you and to share those with others, so they can see just how compassionate He really is.

If you haven't met Him, would you like to? He's already taken the first step and is waiting for you to welcome Him into your life. He's inviting you to receive His forgiveness, step out of the tiny boat you've always been trying to be the captain of, and climb aboard His magnificent luxury liner, where all of the best things of this life and the eternal life to come are to be found. The choice is entirely yours, but I wouldn't wait too long, because this is an offer that does carry an expiration date. If you miss it and depart this earthly life without climbing aboard His ship of Life, it will be forever too late. Forever's a very long time. You don't want to experience forever in the wrong place, without Him, because in that other place, where God isn't, there's no love, no joy, no beauty, no peace, and no life. There's no light and no life there—only darkness, alienation, and suffering. That's how important your decision is. Your whole future depends on this, on what you decide about Him. The stakes are enormous, and God wants you to realize just how high they are and to make the right choice.

Sadly, many people have developed the misconception that God is trying to prevent their happiness and keeps taking away all of the good things they thought should and would be theirs. Their picture of God is a distorted one, so they refuse to connect to Him or to even give Him a chance to show them who He really is. They've placed Him into a tiny box, closed it up, sealed it with heavy-duty packaging tape, and refused to ever open it up again. I picture God shouting at them from inside that tiny box: *"Let Me out! I'm not really in there, although you think I am, and that's all you're going to be able to see of Me until you let Me out of that miniscule box."*

When we begin to walk with Him, He begins to change our hearts. King David, the Psalmist, wrote, *"Create in me a clean heart, O God, and renew a steadfast spirit within me."* (Psalm 51:10 NASB) The Lord described David in Acts 13:22 this way: *"I have found David the son of Jesse, a man after My heart, who will do all My will."* (NASB)

And David was just that type of person. From early childhood on, he sought after God. He pursued Him; he walked with Him; He was instructed by Him; he listened to Him; he fellowshipped with Him; he worshipped Him, and he cried out to Him in times of distress and danger. The Lord always heard David and delivered him. God saw David's heart was totally focused on Him, and, because it was, He knew that He could count on him, raise him up, and entrust the leadership of His people to him. God sent the prophet Samuel to annoint David king over Israel. David was only a young lad at the time, so he would have to wait years and go through many challenges, tests, battles, and much opposition before he would be ready to step into that role as king. God took David from being a shepherd, looking after his father's sheep out in the pasture, to being king and shepherd of His people, the Israelites.

When David arrived to take up his new position, he was ready. God made sure he had learned the important lessons and passed the critical tests; in each test the real issue was, *"David, where is your heart in all of this?"* Most of the time, David's heart was in the right place as he pursued and followed God with all of his passion and strength. The Lord showed David great favor and blessed him. David became a great king, the greatest ruler of Israel who had ever sat on the throne in Jerusalem.

Yet, at times, just as we all experience, David had a heart problem. He allowed his attention to shift from the Lord to someone else. He listened to the wrong voice whispering to him that it was okay to take and sleep with another man's wife. He, David, was king, so he could do whatever he liked. Furthermore, that other man's wife was not only beautiful and desirable, she seemed to be looking in his direction as well. I can imagine David might have thought something like this: *"So, if she wants me, I recognize how desirable she is, and probably her husband doesn't really appreciate her beauty the way I do. I can give her everything she's always dreamed of; it'll be great!"* David listened to the wrong voice. He committed adultery with Bathsheba, who became pregnant with David's child, and, then, David had a huge problem to solve: how to get rid of the complicating, inconvenient truth that Bathsheba was already married.

Bathsheba already had a husband, so David couldn't do the right thing, which would have been the wrong thing, and marry her. He had her husband placed in the front line of battle and instructed his men to fall back, leaving that soldier unprotected. As a result, Uriah, Bathsheba's husband, was killed. David had just committed four grievous sins before the Lord: he lusted, he coveted, he committed adultery, and then he arranged the death of an innocent man— and David was the king! What kind of ruler would steal another man's wife, sleep with her, get her pregnant, and then have the husband killed? If anyone found out, it would be David's head on a platter! You talk about scandal—this was *scandal*! If there had been tabloids back then, the headlines would have all been screaming, *"King Seduces Married Woman—Gets Her Pregnant—Kills Husband!"*

You can be sure that issue would have sold out the moment it hit the streets. People would have been fighting each other just to get their hands on a copy. Talk about a reporter's dream of one day getting the scoop on a big story— this story was huge! If it happened today, this would dominate global news for days on end. Commentators and talk show hosts would have a field day with this. Political pundits would be analyzing every possible angle of the situation and predicting David's imminent downfall.

You can also be sure that a special prosecutor would be swiftly appointed. That investigation would look into, with great detail, everything David had ever thought, imagined, said, or done, and every person he had ever had any connection to, as well as all of his political and financial dealings—in short, everything. That's what special prosecutors are appointed to do: to get to the bottom of something. In most cases, it appears that they do just that: they focus on the specific issue and scope of investigation at hand. Other times, however, one might be forgiven for beginning to wonder if a completely different agenda might not be driving the whole thing. Let's just leave it at that. History will one day sort it all out, just as it did in King David's day.

The real truth will come out, because, sooner or later, it always does. That's the wonderful thing about truth: you can't control it. You can try to spin it, distort it, manipulate it, ignore it, or even bury it, but you can't kill it. Truth always wins out; it always prevails in the end—always. Each of us will have to decide where we're going to place our bets: on the side of truth, or on the opposite side.

Winston Churchill once said something that I think is one of the most brilliant observations of all time concerning this particularly puzzling aspect of the human condition: *"Men occasionally stumble over the truth, but most of them pick themselves up and hurry off, as if nothing had happened."*[1] I love that quote. It is, and always will be, one of my absolute favorites.

Has that ever happened to you? Have you ever stumbled over the truth—run into it—maybe even tripped over it—or perhaps it even knocked you flat on your back— but then you picked yourself up and hurried off, as if nothing had happened? I know I have, and I suspect we all have. What is it about truth that makes it so difficult for us to acknowledge it? Have you ever thought about that? Why do we go to such great lengths to ignore or deny truth and keep it at arm's length? What is it about truth that is so threatening to us?

Truth always demands a response. Whether we bump into it, stumble over it, or even crash into it—which happens when God is really trying to get our attention, it is presenting itself to us and demanding a response. If we pretend we haven't even encountered it, however, there will be no effect: there will be no recognition on our part that something significant has taken place. Thus, that moment of opportunity to learn and change something will be lost—perhaps forever. We might be given another moment of truth, because God is merciful and understands our fallen nature and weakness without Him, but that particular window of opportunity for God to really meet us and help us step out of our old and into His new has already shut. It closed, because we failed to recognize and see it as an invitation. It shut, because we chose to ignore it and discarded it as something not worthy of attention. We might be shocked when we meet the Lord at the end of our lives and see just how many such missed truth moments we failed to grasp.

Truth does indeed demand a response. For nearly ten months before I went to attend that two-week international convocation and prayer tour in Israel, the Lord had been speaking to me about a particular heart issue. He gave me a number of chances to examine what I was doing, to turn away from it, and to surrender that part of myself to Him completely. I remember a few occasions when He asked me in my spirit, *"What are you doing? What are you looking for here?"* At times, I listened and heeded Him, but then there were other times when I didn't. What was the heart issue about which He was confronting me?

It is what others have described as *an ungodly soul tie*. This is any kind of emotional, physical, mental, financial, or even spiritual attachment to another person that contains impure, selfish intentions on our part or theirs in some way. It develops because we are focused only on ourself and what we want, rather than considering what is best for the other person as well—thus, it is not of the Lord. He cannot bless it, nor will He, if it is not rooted primarily in His unconditional, sacrificial love. He will only ask us to surrender it and turn it over to Him.

I did turn away from that ungodly soul tie sometimes, but, at other times, I wanted to go back to it. That process shouldn't have lasted ten months; it should have only taken ten seconds. It was my decision to keep revisiting it, yet, the Lord, in His great mercy and compassion, kept giving me another chance to resolve to let go of it. He also let me know that, if I continued to ignore His warnings, He would have nothing new for me there in Jerusalem at the 2018 Convocation. It was at that point that I made the decision to confess the issue to two brothers, turned back to God, and received His forgiveness and restoration.

When we are a single or even married person of faith, there are deep desires and longings within us that are very powerful. God placed these deep yearnings for closeness within us so we could some day experience full intimacy on all levels with the person we will choose to commit ourself to in marriage for the rest of our life. Yet, sometimes, in a moment of weakness or distraction, we let our guard down and take a step in the wrong direction. When we do that, the enemy is always there, attempting to ambush us and to deceive us into rationalizing our decision.

This is what the enemy's voice can sound like: *"Oh, it's no big deal. God will understand. He'll forgive you; He always does. Stop resisting; just let yourself go."*

Unmet emotional and physical needs are powerful, just as powerful as an ocean tidal wave. If we're not careful and get too close, they can sweep us away from a place of safety in the Lord and engulf our whole being; they can even destroy us. That's how serious this issue is. God wants us to recognize and avoid the potential danger and use the spiritual intelligence and wisdom He has already given us.

The Lord mercifully put up roadblocks that kept me from taking any definite steps in the wrong direction, but there were moments when a part of me strongly desired to pursue that selfish soul tie. It was only through God's grace that I didn't. The fact that I didn't, doesn't mean that I didn't. In the physical world, I didn't take a wrong step, but in my heart, I did—many times. God looks at the heart, and if we do something at the heart level, He counts it as if we had actually committed that thing. That's why purity of heart is of such great importance to Him. If it is such a key issue to Him, it should be to us as well.

Our former American Vice-President, Mike Pence, said, in an interview years ago, that he would never have dinner alone with any woman who wasn't his wife. Immediately after sharing that, the Vice-President was ridiculed and attacked by many for being hopelessly old-fashioned and out of touch with the modern world. I'm sure that many people who heard him make that statement thought it was strange, because in our modern society today almost anything goes. There are fewer and fewer moral standards and Biblical values which, not so long ago, used to be the standards that we lived by. Yet, was what Vice-President Pence said really all that strange?

If we know that certain situations might be problematic, could cause us to fall into temptation, or that other people might get the wrong idea if they saw us alone with someone who isn't our spouse, it's just best to avoid those situations as much as we can. This is even more important if we find ourself in a position of leadership at any level, because there is always someone paying attention to our actions. If they see us do something, they may assume it's okay and will follow our example. We bear great responsibility for the standards we set for others.

If you're a married man or woman, you need to think very carefully about the situations you place yourself in when there's a person of the opposite sex involved. Even if you had never thought of going in the wrong direction, there is always the possibility that, if you find yourself alone with that other person who is not your spouse, and some kind of deeper emotional, physical, or even spiritual connection develops toward them, you could, even against your better judgment and determination, be swept away by that emotional or physical tidal wave, especially if you and the other person have significant unmet emotional, physical or intellectual needs and the two of you connect on some deeper level. That sudden bonding can become explosive—out of control, and it can overwhelm a person in a split second.

This is not the material of a romance novel; this is what happens in real life, and it probably occurs a lot more often than we think it does. God wants to protect us from this kind of thing ever happening to us, because He knows the disastrous level of damage it can do to our heart, to others, to our testimony, to our destiny, and to His reputation. The guilt and confusion that can occur after we fall into something like this can hijack, derail, or even destroy any authentic deeper emotions that we might otherwise desire to express to someone we truly love or to whom we are committed.

If we do miss the mark and fall into a situation like the one I've described above, there is always deliverance, forgiveness and restoration from the Lord, if we are quick to confess it, turn away from it, and accept responsibility for what we've done. We will experience His forgiveness and restoration, but, depending on the seriousness of the situation, there may very well be consequences that we will have to face, because it is through those that God will help us recognize the real cost of taking a severe misstep in the wrong direction. There is always a price to pay when we miss the mark, and the greater the miss, the greater the consequences. He will give us grace, to the extent He sees that our failure was just a one-time mistake on our part, and that in our heart we have resolved to give the whole thing over to Him and determine to never go there again.

King David paid an enormous price for his moral failure. His baby with Bathsheba was still-born. God told David that, because of what he had done, and the fact that he had an innocent man's blood on his hands, David would not be allowed to build His House, a Temple, for the Lord, something David had longed to accomplish to honor God. That task would be given to David's son, Solomon. There would be other consequences as well.

What are the lessons here for us? I believe there are several:

First: What we see as just little things are not little at all; in fact, to God, they are very big things. It's the little things in our lives that determine what kinds of larger things we will grow and what He will be able to do in and through us.

Second: If we hear the Lord asking us, *"What are you doing?"* we need to immediately stop—right then and there, and allow Him to take inventory of our heart. There's no guarantee that He will speak to us about that issue again. Sometimes He will, but if He sees that we're determined to have our own way rather than His much better, higher path, He may just say to us, *"your will be done,"* and allow us to experience the fruit of that choice.

Third: His Heart is pure and perfect; He wants to help us develop a heart that is as pure as His. Our level of intimacy with God depends entirely on how clean our heart is before Him. There are things He plans and longs to release to and through us, but until we determine to pursue His heart with all of our intention and will, what He can share with us and do through us will be limited—not by Him—but by us.

Fourth: If we still have any areas of our lives which are not fully surrendered to God, the promise of His total protection is limited. He can, and will still protect us, because of His great love, but the real problem here is that those unsurrendered areas give the enemy access into those sections of our lives.

There are two kingdoms at work here, where we live. The one is the kingdom of darkness. In that kingdom, which is already a judged and defeated one—a realm that will one day very soon be destroyed and annihilated forever—the ruler's modus operandi is: *"The thief comes only to steal, and kill, and destroy."* (John 10:10 NASB)

In the other one, the only real, lasting Kingdom, the perfect King's modus operandi is: *"I came that they might have life, and might have it abundantly."* (John 10:10 NASB) That's a shockingly stark contrast!

I believe that God is asking us, every moment of every day, *"What do you want?"* Everything, and I mean everything, depends on our answer to that question. Speaking in His name here, I would like to ask you: *What is it that you want? What do you really want?*

If it's more of Him, He longs to and will give you the best future imaginable—in fact, way beyond your ability to contemplate. That's how good He is and what your future with Him will look like if you do life His way. If you prefer, however, to continue going your own way, running your own life, and being your own captain, God will allow you to do that, because He always respects our choices.

Sometimes, I'm really glad He's given us free will, but, to be honest, there have been a few times when I've asked Him why He didn't just make us all obedient and pure in heart, so we wouldn't have to make all of these difficult choices. One thing I am really thankful about is that God doesn't just let us get away with things. He's the ultimate good Parent, which means that, out of His infinite love and mercy towards us, He stops us, confronts us, speaks to us, questions us, and corrects us when He sees us wanting or starting to take a step in the wrong direction. That's exactly what a good parent does: he or she intervenes at a teachable moment or crossroads of decision to form the child's character and to help them understand the issue at hand and the importance of making a good choice. The good parent is always there helping to guide the child, so that he or she will mature, realize that he or she is responsible for his or her own actions, and that **decisions decide destiny**. The good parent wants, with all of his or her heart, to give that child a good future and a hope. That is precisely what God desires for each of us— exactly that, but we have to choose it.

Our Heavenly Father knows that purity of heart, available through His Son Jesus' sacrifice on the cross, is what connects our heart to His and what makes it possible for Him to develop an exemplary character in us. Purity of heart is also the key which helps us create strong, beautiful, faithful, and lasting relationships rooted in His love and goodness.

Jesus Himself said, *"Blessed are the pure in heart, for they shall see God."* (Matthew 5:8 NASB)

To see God means to experience Him, to know Him, to develop in intimacy with Him, and to have Him actively present in our lives, relationships, activities, and service to Him and others.

So, when Jesus said this, I believe what He was really asking us was, *"Just how much of a relationship with Me do you really want? I've taken the first step toward you. Now, what do **you** want?"*

Purity of heart is at the very center of all of life; that's why the Lord is asking each of us to take it seriously. Everything, and I mean **everything** depends on how undefiled our heart is before Him.

Watch over your heart with all diligence,
For from it flow the springs of life. (Proverbs 4:23 NASB)

Chapter 18: Emotional Processing For Guys

For most, if not all males, the female heart is a beautiful, yet mysterious wonder of great sensitivity and compassion, which is why it takes a man a whole lifetime, or whatever amount of time he is given, to study the heart of the woman he loves: to learn about her and to discover how to appreciate, honor, support, and bless her. Although he will never fully understand her in all of her amazing complexity, if he remains committed to discovering her and what she needs, his love and appreciation for her will continue to deepen and grow over the years.

Security on all levels, but especially emotional security, is a woman's greatest and most important emotional need. If she doesn't feel emotionally, physically, financially and spiritually secure with a man, she won't be able to truly love him or feel strong bonds towards him. If this basic need of hers to experience security from the man she loves isn't met, she will feel that she can't and daren't trust him with this deepest part of herself—where she is the most vulnerable and can thus be the most easily hurt, disappointed, wounded, or betrayed.

Like everything else in life, if something is important to us, we will recognize its value and choose to invest in it. This is especially true when it comes to a man and how he chooses to relate to the emotions and heart of the woman he loves. If he is wise, he will make this a priority and learn to understand, translate, and communicate with her in her own heart language. It's not enough to just pay attention to her heart; you have to learn how to respond in such a way that she feels you have listened to her and tried to understand her. It's your *willingness* to engage in the conversation and invest in the relationship that is important to her. The more you engage and invest, the more she will open up and share with you what's really going on inside of her. It's not a failure if you don't understand her yet; the important thing is that you genuinely *want* to understand her and that you are fully involved in and committed to this process. She'll detect very quickly if you aren't sincere, so be honest: the future of your relationship depends on this.

As you are engaged in studying her, here are some questions to look at concerning your own emotions and how they develop:

- Do your feelings usually begin to emerge first as a result of a physical attraction to her? To what extent? How would you describe those feelings?
- Do your feelings tend to develop first as a result of what she says to you, how she says it, and how she expresses herself? What are those feelings?

- How often do your emotions toward her surface while you are doing an activity, participating in a program, or attending an event together? What do those feelings look like?
- If spending time with her is how your feelings more typically begin to develop, does the opposite also occur? So, when you are not with her, do your feelings about her begin to diminish? To what extent? How important to you is her physical presence in terms of your being able to feel something emotionally significant toward her?
- Do you ever develop emotions toward her as a result of a spiritual experience you shared together, such as praying, worshipping, or studying God's Word? In what ways was that spiritually-based emotional experience different for you?
- Do your feelings about her ever emerge because you share similar ideas, values, beliefs, or experiences concerning important life issues?
- Do your emotions ever begin to develop as a result of how attentively, actively, empathetically, acceptingly, and carefully she listens to you? How does that make you feel?
- Do your feelings ever begin to develop because of how she expresses her emotions to or with you, either in words or in some kind of emotional or physical response? What do you feel in those situations?
- How easy is it for you to freely express your emotions to her when you are together? Is there any area of your emotions that you are unwilling or unable to express to her? Which one/s? Any idea why that is, or what might be blocking or preventing you from openly expressing to her how you really feel?
- How easy is it for you to talk about your emotions with her, even when it's directly about her? How comfortable are you doing that in writing or while talking on the phone?
- Are there any areas of your emotions that for you remain a mystery (you don't understand where they come from, when they might appear, or what you should do with them)?
- In thinking about this other person right now, how do you feel? What emotions are present or beginning to surface?
- If you knew that this would or might possibly be the last time you would ever see her or communicate with her, what would you most want to say? Is there anything you would want to make sure she knows?
- Have you sensed the Lord showing or teaching you anything in the area of your emotions, either in the recent situations of your life or right now? Do you sense Him inviting you to do or to change something in any of these areas?
- What question/s would you ask the Lord about all of this if He were sitting right there next to you now? What do you think He would say in reply?
- What question/s do you think the Lord would ask you if He were sitting right there next to you about all of this? What do you think you would say to Him?
- As a spiritual exercise, take a few minutes now or as soon as you have at least an hour of free, undisturbed time alone. Take out your Bible, a pad of paper and a pen, and sit quietly before the Lord. Focus on the two previous questions. Ask the Lord to come and sit with you. Write down and share with Him whatever is on

your heart, invite Him to do the same, then write down everything that takes place. Allow Him to meet you right where you are and to minister to you: He longs to do that. He will bless this time that you have set apart to discover more about your emotions: where they come from; how they develop; what they mean, and what to do with them.

May God richly guide and bless you as you spend time with Him exploring this key aspect of your inner life.

Chapter 19: The Way Back Home

God is a lover, in fact He is *the Lover*, the origin of love and compassion.

God is love, and the one who abides in love abides in God, and God abides in Him. (1ˢᵗ John 4:16 NASB)

God relentlessly pursues us with His love. He will follow us to the ends of the earth and to the end of time itself with His love. We cannot even begin to fathom the depths of His passion for us. When we look at love Incarnate, Jesus, we see what love really looks like. Love is made visible through what love does. Love is not just a series of nice words on paper, nor is it just a collection of warm feelings in the heart; it is so much more than that.

As important as words and feelings, especially sanctified feelings, are, love is not based just on words or on emotions. Words and feelings come and go. Sometimes we have words to express to someone how we feel about them, yet, at other times we do not. There are occasions when we experience deeper feelings of love toward someone, however, at other times those feelings are absent. Does that mean that we don't really love them?

Love costs something; sometimes, it costs everything. Love is simple; it is not easy. Love is what makes or breaks us in the end. We either love and grow, or we refuse to love and slowly die. It's that serious a matter. Love invites a response. We can choose to ignore it, but that doesn't change the fact that love is still there, knocking on our door, and waiting for us to open our heart. When we respond, love expands our whole being and our capacity to love. There's a wonderful quote by Ulrich Schaffer: "*Love is not the feeling of a moment, but the conscious decision for a way of life.*"[1]

As I was lying in bed early one November 2018 morning, pouring my heart out to the Lord, and asking Him to help me understand something from His perspective and to speak to me about that, I began to ask Him how in the world He can continue to pursue and love us with such passion and determination, when He knows that there are some people who will never allow themselves to be touched or changed by His love. He already knows that they will continue to pursue other things and will ignore Him and all that He is offering them. How can He continue to love all of us, when so much of the time there is little or no response on our part, or the response is so half-hearted that it must surely break His heart? Can God's heart really be broken? I don't know, but His heart can be grieved. I regret that there have been many times in my life when I have sorrowed Him. Even though I knew He was reaching out to me, I turned to other things and people rather than to Him.

God never gives up on us; He doesn't. We may turn away from Him, but He never turns from us. Even when we step away from Him, He continues to reach out toward us and invites us to come back and return home to Him. I invite you to go back and read the story of the prodigal son again. In that parable, the younger son brashly demands his inheritance, which should only rightfully become his after his father passes away. After he receives it, he then goes out into the world to eat, drink, be merry, and enjoy all the world has to offer. What is the father doing the entire time the younger son is away partying and doing his thing without any concern for how his actions and choices are affecting others?

The father is waiting, praying, and hoping—hoping that someday, somewhere, the moment will come when his younger son will awaken from his drunken stupor of temporary pleasures, come to his senses, realize what a huge mistake he has made, and make his way back home to his father's house.

The father in that story has not written the younger son off; he has not crossed him off his list; he has not judged or condemned him; he has not shut him out of his heart; he has not disinherited him; he has not thought the worst of him, nor has he forgotten about him. On the contrary, he continues to hope for and seek a full restoration of that broken relationship, although there is no guarantee his younger son will ever make the decision to return.

Through the example of the father in that story, our Heavenly Father is again showing me that love is a choice. After you remove everything else from the picture and the equation, it all comes down to this: who and what will we choose? Everything depends upon our choices. God has already made His determination: He has chosen us, and He doesn't regret His decision; He has said yes to us. As powerful, infinite, loving, kind-hearted, merciful, gentle, righteous, and holy as He is, there is one thing, however, that is impossible for Him to do, and that is to choose for us.

He has given us free will––the ability to make our own choices freely without any pressure from Him. God will guide us in our decisions if we invite Him to do so, and He will work through all of our choices, both the good and the bad ones, to ultimately bring good out of every situation, if we commit ourself and our way to Him. Even though He knows in advance what an unfavorable decision on our part will result in, we are free to make the wrong choice. This is where it can become very difficult for God, and for us.

Choices can be challenging, even when we are seeking God about what to do. We want to know we are making the right decision when we have to choose; God wants that too. He wants to help us make a wise choice, a good choice, a heart-informed choice, a healthy choice, a life-affirming choice, and a choice that honors Him and the best of what He has placed in us. At every crossroads of decision, He will guide us if we will turn to Him and commit ourself to Him. God alone can see clearly which way we should go. I believe that He wants us to freely choose Him, each and every time, above everything and everyone else. He wants us to make the best decision far more than we do. Can you imagine that? God has a much greater desire for us to make the best possible choice than we do; that is very comforting to know! It's also very reassuring to realize that He is with us in every detail of our deliberations. Even when we don't feel His presence, He is still active in that process to work, guide, and arrange circumstances, based on what we have chosen and the intention of our heart toward Him.

Many years ago, when I had resigned my first job as a YMCA Professional Director after three years of wonderful, very intensive employment because I had reached a point of feeling burned out, I returned to my home state of Pennsylvania and spent several months seeking direction. During that break, I took a six-month temporary position at a social agency. Toward the end of that period, I realized that I really wanted to continue in YMCA work, and I felt the Lord was guiding me to pursue that direction, so I started to look for YMCA openings in different parts of the country.

Shortly thereafter, two positions were advertised in the YMCA National Vacancy List, and both looked interesting, so I applied for them. One of them was a higher position at the YMCA I had just left, and the other, a position at a YMCA in the state of Connecticut. I updated my resumé, composed a cover letter tailored to each position, and sent those off by post. A few weeks later, I received an invitation to go for an interview at the YMCA in Connecticut and was also offered the position at my previous YMCA. The interview went well, and not long after I had returned home again, I received a call from the Executive Director of that institution. He offered me the job, and I asked him if I could have a few days to think things over, as I was also considering the position at my previous YMCA. He agreed.

I began asking the Lord to show me which of those two positions He desired me to accept. I earnestly wanted to know which direction He intended for me, and I was ready to follow that. I was seeking Him by listening, reading Scripture, praying, and searching but still had no clear guidance. Finally, the day arrived when I would have to call back the Director of the Connecticut YMCA and give him an answer. I was in complete turmoil, because I had no idea what to do. I wanted to make the better choice, but I still had no sense of which position to accept, even though I had made lists—comparing and contrasting the benefits and drawbacks of each choice. I had also solicited advice from several godly people whose wisdom I respected, yet, I hadn't received any clear direction from God.

Later that morning, I told my mother I was going out to the woods to be alone with the Lord: to read His Word, to pray, listen, and discover what He wanted me to do. I headed off, drove about 40 minutes to a place which overlooked the river, and walked through the woods to a lookout point which had a great view. I spent the whole day there seeking, praying, fasting, listening, and reading Scripture. Finally, the sun was beginning to set, and I still hadn't received an answer. I was beginning to feel desperate. *Lord, I have committed this choice to You and have asked You to show me which way to go. I need to hear from You, right now. Please show me what to do: I want to make the right choice here. Thank you!*

In that frame of mind, and with a heavy heart, I returned home. My mother, who was also the associate pastor of a local church, was waiting for me with a delicious dinner and a listening ear. I shared the situation with her and asked her what God was doing and why He wasn't giving me clear direction when He knew I had committed my decision to Him. Why was He silent? And then, my mother said something that completely challenged my theology and made me question my mother's understanding of who God is and how He operates. Here is what she said to me, and I will never forget it.

"You have asked God with all of your heart to give you an answer about this, and still He has not, though you have been intensely seeking Him for clear direction. He knows your heart and that you want to honor and obey Him in this. I think here, God is asking you to choose, and He will be pleased with whichever choice you make."

Right there, I interrupted my mother and asked her, *Why would He do that? Why would He ask me to choose, when I don't know what the right choice is? He knows what the right decision is here, yet He isn't telling me anything. Why not? Doesn't He care about me? Doesn't He want me to make the right choice? These two positions have dissimilar profiles and are in very different parts of the country. One of these has to be the right path, and the other, the wrong one. I need to know what the right choice is, because that's the one I want to accept.*

Once again, my mother tried to explain to me what she thought the situation was really about: *"As we mature in the Lord, He teaches us how to make wise, sound decisions that honor Him, are pleasing to Him, and in agreement with His will. We always need to ask for His guidance and direction. There are times He will give us a very clear indication, yet, other times, He will seem to remain silent. In those situations, He is asking us to step out in faith, to trust Him unreservedly, and to ask Him to direct our steps. It is an invitation to get to know Him on a deeper level."*

I heard my mother's words, and I understood their meaning, yet, I had absolutely no idea what she was talking about. I highly respected my mother, her godly wisdom, and life experience. Until that point, the advice she had shared with me had almost always been right. This time, however, I wasn't so sure. *Is my mother in error here? How could God possibly be asking me to choose? He doesn't work like that, and I don't want to make a huge mistake. I am still asking Him to show me which job to accept.*

I waited another hour or so, but there was no answer from the Lord. I had promised to call the Directors of both YMCAs back with an answer that evening, and it was already 8:00 p.m.. With a very heavy, conflicted heart, I picked up the phone and dialed the number of the YMCA in Connecticut. In that moment, I again asked the Lord to guide me, as I had decided to turn down that position. Then, something very strange occurred. In the middle of the conversation, the Director of that YMCA paused and asked me, *"So, what have you decided?"* I hesitated for a few seconds, fully intending to politely turn down his offer, and said, *You know, this has been an extremely difficult decision for me. I've spent the whole day seeking God and asking Him to guide me—and what I have decided is—to accept your offer.*

As soon as those words left my mouth, I was shocked! I had fully intended to turn that position down! Those weren't even my words, so whose were they? Where did those sentences come from? Immediately, I tried to come up with a way to explain that I didn't mean what I had said, but I couldn't think of a way to logically explain that to that gentleman, so I didn't. He told me he was delighted that I would soon be joining their staff team and wished me the very best as I prepared to relocate there and assume my new duties at their organization.

At that point, my heart was even heavier, and I felt even more confused than I had felt all day while seeking the Lord and asking Him for direction. I had no idea what was happening, but I had to call my former boss at the other YMCA back and give him the news that I wouldn't be returning to work there. I dialed that number, my former boss answered, and, after I told him what had happened, he replied: *"I'm really sorry to hear you won't be returning, because you were, and would continue to be, a great asset to our organization. I was really looking forward to your coming back as my new Associate Executive Director. I also see, however, that you're at a point now where you really need something totally new—a fresh challenge and different experiences, so I think this is really the best choice for you."*

As he spoke those words, I felt even worse and thought I had made an even greater mistake. He was the kind of person I would really have enjoyed working for again, and I was very much in agreement with his vision for the future of that YMCA. While I tried to gather my words together, I thanked him for his understanding, told him I wasn't sure I had made the right decision, and wished him and the organization the very best.

Then, I went back downstairs to the kitchen and tried to explain to my mother what had just happened. She didn't say much but affirmed me in the decision I had just made. She reminded me that she loved me, that she fully supported me in that choice, and that God would help me to find my way in that new employment situation.

If anyone had said to me right then that God works in mysterious ways, I would have said, *No, He doesn't. He works in crazy ways!*

A few weeks later, after I had arrived at that Connecticut YMCA and met the staff, I walked into my new office, and the first thing I noticed on the desk was a gorgeous bouquet of fresh flowers with a note attached. I went over to the bouquet, opened the note, and this is what was written in it:*"With our warmest, very best wishes for success in your new position there!"(the name of the Executive Director of my former YMCA)*

I immediately closed the door to my office, sat down in the chair, and started weeping. I don't know how long I sat there, but it was more than a few minutes. That incredibly kind, generous gesture from my former boss, the person I had just said no to regarding what would have certainly been a wonderful career advancement opportunity, was one of the most affirming and touching moments of my entire life, and I will never forget that.

I felt two things in that moment: one, a sense of further regret that I had turned that job offer down, and two—paradoxically, a sense of freedom. In receiving that kind gesture of affirmation from my former boss, I also felt free to step fully into that new position and leave the previous one behind.

My former supervisor showed me such wonderful graciousness in that moment, and to this day I carry within me that same understanding towards others; grace which originates from the Father's heart of love for each of us.

Sometimes, we have no idea why we make a choice; we just know we have to choose. The encouraging thing in all of this is, that if we have committed our decision to God and are depending on Him, He will bring good of that, and He will bring us safely and successfully to the amazing and glorious destiny He has designed and purposed for us. That is *good news!*

Now, many years later, as I look back on that career move and what followed, I can see how marvelously God's Hand was guiding me, though I couldn't see or understand what He was doing at that time. It was only toward the end of those six and a half wonderful years at that Connecticut YMCA that the Lord opened an opportunity through our affiliated YMCA resident camp to accompany a group of seventeen teens from two YMCAs to a three-week international camp, Camp Csilleberc, just north of Budapest, Hungary. That is how the Lord arranged my steps to bring me to the next place He had purposed for me to serve Him. I had no idea back then that I would be returning to Hungary after those three weeks at Csilleberc, let alone for a period of 25 years—years which have been among the most beautiful, instructive, challenging, and productive of my entire life.

If you find yourself in a valley of decision and have absolutely no idea what you want or should do; if you have no understanding of what God is doing or plans to do; if you know that you desire with all of your heart to love, serve, honor, and follow Him: keep listening, keep seeking, keep asking, keep following, and keep trusting Him. Be assured that He can and will order your steps to guide you into the fullness of your inheritance in Him, which is unimaginably glorious and good.

The steps of a man are established by the Lord; And He delights in his way. (Psalm 37:23 NASB)

Chapter 20: Just Trust

When you begin to love someone with all of your heart, you are entering into one of the most beautiful, transformative, yet challenging places imaginable. You are embarking upon a journey which offers no guarantees whatsoever—nothing, except the certainty that you have chosen to love another person unreservedly, and that you long to experience all that God has to offer to both of you.

If the two of you are in the same place and care for each other at the same level, you are greatly blessed, because you are already beginning to explore the possibilities of a life together. If, however, the other person is not at the place where they see and love you the way you love them, your journey is going to be very different and a much more difficult one.

If you are in that place where love is not yet reciprocal, but you know that you have been called to love that other person, and that there has been placed such a deep, strong, and unconditional love for them within you that nothing could ever shake it, you are also greatly blessed. That kind of love only originates from the heart of the Father: this is the way that He loves us. You've been given the special burden of expressing love, even though you have no idea whether or not that love will ever be felt, desired, or returned by the other person. Yet, you—you have chosen to love.

That is all that you can do: to love them, to listen, to wait, and to see. It's as if your heart is the precious cargo on a large ship having launched out into the deep—into the middle of the ocean, and the ship is just sailing, but there's still no port or harbor to receive your cargo. You just have to keep sailing, looking, and waiting, until the destination becomes clear. During that time, I sense the Lord may be saying to you, *"Give Me your precious cargo; let Me hold it securely for you in My strong, loving arms, until it finds the perfect place I have destined for it to be received."*

That can be a very tough place to be, especially if it is for a longer period of time. Imagine that you are Abram. You know that God has called you to set out on a journey to an unknown destination, and He's shown you something so incredibly amazing about your future that you can scarcely dare to believe it. Yet, unlike Abram, you're on this journey alone, so, it's just you and the Lord. You set out, because you've heard His voice, you know He's in this, and you realize that your destiny now lies in a new, unexplored direction. Only God knows where you're headed; only He has the roadmap, but He isn't showing it to you. He just says, *"Come! Follow Me! This way! Keep coming! Trust Me! I know the Way!"*

At first, the expedition seems exciting, even exhilarating. It's all new, fresh, and stimulating, and you begin to get a taste of the great adventure that lies ahead. Then, a bit further along the way, you suddenly find yourself in the middle of a vast desert: a place bitterly inhospitable to human life, unless you know what to expect and have prepared carefully for how to proceed through it. So, there you are, trekking through the miles and miles of sand—only sand—hardly a trace of life anywhere. After a while, your shoes begin to wear out, so you take them off. Now you're walking on the hot sand in your bare feet, trying to keep moving quickly enough so the soles of your feet don't get burned. The noonday sun begins to feel so scorchingly hot that even the hat on your head doesn't really offer much protection, and you begin to feel tired, discouraged, and very alone. You thought you had heard His voice at the beginning of this journey, but He hasn't said much to you since you entered this desert, and now you are wondering where He is. "Why isn't He saying anything to me? Is this some kind of test?"

Being alone in the desert can play tricks on your senses. You begin to hear, see, and feel things, and you're not quite sure if they're real or if you're just imagining them. Sometimes, you think you see an oasis just up ahead, but as you get closer, you realize it was just a mirage. That's what happens when you're out in the desert for a while: your sense of reality begins to become distorted, and you start to lose energy, strength, and hope. *"How long is this desert, anyway? Where does it end? Will it end? Is there an oasis somewhere along the way? My water bottle's down to the last few drops and I'm really getting thirsty—never imagined I'd be in a place without water for so long. How much further can I go on like this? What if there is no water source up ahead—then what? Will I make it? Are you still with me, Lord?"*

Then, you start to lose your balance, your footing becomes unstable, and you fall down. You pull yourself up again and try to keep going, but it's becoming more difficult. The loss of footing and falling down become more and more frequent, and, then, you're at the point where you feel like just giving up, because you can't see a way out of the desert. This is becoming too hard, and there's no destination in sight. Your perspective has changed from dreaming and hoping about the good future God had showed you, to just survival.

Many of you have been in this kind of place at some point of your life; so have I. In fact, for me, it was just recently. I never imagined that I would be in that kind of place again, but, I was, and I had no idea what to do when I found myself there. I knew that God was guiding me, that He was speaking to me, and that He had a plan, but I didn't see a way forward. I was beginning to lose hope, focus, and perspective. I didn't understand what He was doing, and I needed reassurance from Him to help me keep going, walking, moving forward, hoping, and trusting that He was still in the process. I needed to believe that He would bring good out of it at some point, in some way, for me, as well as for someone I care deeply about, and that He would be honored and glorified in it all.

Faith is not faith unless it is tested. You can receive a word from the Lord, a wonderful, powerful, life-changing word, but, as soon as you do, you should know that it is going to be tested. Testing shakes out all of the unnecessary baggage and debris that don't belong in us, and it forces us to dig deeply down inside to trust Him like we've never done so before. That's what He's always asking us to do in every situation of life—to just trust Him: to trust Him, whether we see something or not; to trust Him, whether we feel something or not; to trust Him, whether we understand something or not; to trust Him, whether we receive something or not; to trust Him, regardless of what is happening around or within us.

Trust is the foundation of relationship and faith. Without it, nothing can take root and grow. You either trust, or you don't; there's no middle ground. It's either say yes to trust, or say no. Trust doesn't give us the option of being half-in or half-out; it's either all-in, or all-out.

When we choose to trust Him, He can open doors that would remain closed forever otherwise. When we choose to trust Him, He can change or rearrange circumstances. When we choose to trust Him, He can change our heart. When we choose to trust Him, He can even change another's heart. He can do anything, if we will just choose to trust Him. Trust, like love, is simple but not easy.

That's the lesson for all us here: to just place our confidence in Him, no matter what is going on in our life or what we are struggling with, because we're all wrestling with something. Take the risk of launching out into the deep, and abandon yourself to the One who alone is the Captain of all of our ships and the precious cargo He has placed there. He alone has the precise navigational charts for your voyage and for mine. He alone knows where the icebergs are which could sink our ships halfway across the ocean, and He alone is able to carefully steer us away from them. We can trust Him, and Him alone, to bring us safely, wholly, and successfully through every storm and circumstance—safely through, to the glorious and marvelous destiny He has purposed for each and every one of us.

Just trust. That's all we need to do today, and every day, for the rest of our days along this earthly part of our eternal journey in Him.

Trust in the Lord, and do good; Dwell in the land and cultivate faithfulness.
Delight yourself in the Lord; And He will give you the desires of your heart.
Commit your way to the Lord, Trust also in Him, and He will do it. (Psalm 37:3–5 NASB)

Chapter 21: Thanksgiving Heart

In everything give thanks; for this is God's will for you in Christ Jesus. (1st Thessalonians: 5:18 NASB)

In every situation of life, we are always given two choices: to thank God for His goodness, faithfulness, protection, provision, mercy, and deliverance in that situation, or to step away from the position of trusting Him and focus on our circumstances rather than on Him.

In 1st Thessalonians 5:18, He doesn't instruct us to give thanks *for* the situation, but rather to give thanks *in* the situation. When we do that, we are confessing and declaring that He is Sovereign over all—over everything—including whatever present circumstance we may find ourself in.

Choosing to cultivate a thankful heart is really a moment-by-moment decision. It takes practice, and, like anything else in life, it requires awareness and a clear intention in what we are thinking, feeling, and choosing.

God wants us to develop and live out of a heart of such overwhelming thanksgiving and praise to Him that we will experience more and more of the very fullness of His presence and glory in our lives. He wants to demonstrate His goodness, no matter what is going on around us. The more we choose to thank Him, the more He will release the abundance of every good thing He has planned and purposed for us.

Our choices of whether or not to thank Him every day not only affect us, our destiny in Him, and those within our circle of influence, they also serve as a powerful witness to others who are reading the open book of our lives to see whether the things we say we believe, we really believe.

Let's begin each new day with a heart of thanksgiving and praise to the One who lavishes upon us His infinite, unconditional, and incomparable love.

My list of reasons to thank and praise God:

- He's the Designer and Creator of all.
- He loves us.
- He has redeemed us.
- He cares for us.
- He's good.
- He'll never leave or forsake us.
- He's totally reliable.

- If we trust God, He can and will bring good out of every situation.
- He's given us hundreds of fabulous promises.
- He's the God of second chances.
- He is love.
- He has a unique, amazing mission and destiny for each of us.
- He's given us the privilege of partnering with Him.
- His plans for our life are perfect—much better than our own.
- He reigns forevermore in glory, majesty, power, righteousness, goodness, and justice.
- He never changes but is always doing something new, creative, and totally out-of-the-box amazing.
- He's the God of new beginnings.
- He's generous and bountiful; we can't outgive Him.
- His economic system works perfectly: nothing is ever wasted, and everything that can be used again is recycled.
- He loves to surprise us with good things.
- His strength always carries us through.
- He's perfect.
- He's not only Master of the big picture, He's also interested and involved in every detail.
- He doesn't give up on us, even though we sometimes feel like giving up on ourself.
- He's not only given us Himself but also His Guidebook and manual for successful living, which, if followed carefully and faithfully, is guaranteed to never fail.

Chapter 22: Blessing Over Your Beloved

I bless every thought you take.
I bless each decision you make.
I bless every breath you breathe.
I bless each truth you receive.
I bless every word you say.
I bless each prayer you pray.
I bless every place you go.
I bless each seed you sow.
I bless every person you meet.
I bless each problem you defeat.
I bless every step of your race.
I bless each challenge you embrace.
I bless every hand you hold.
I bless each heart you enfold.
I bless every kindness you impart.
I bless each longing of your heart.
I bless you to shine in His light.
I bless you to stand in His might.
I bless you to live from above.
I bless you to walk in His love.
I bless each moment of your day.
I bless you to walk in His way.
I bless you.

Chapter 23: A Prayer For Your Heart

Lord, I ask You to please grant me today

- a joyful heart
- a thankful heart
- an open heart
- a responsive heart
- a listening heart
- a faithful heart
- an obedient heart
- a willing heart
- a co-operative heart
- a positive heart
- an enthusiastic heart
- an adventurous heart
- a loving heart
- an aware heart
- a pure heart
- a seeking heart
- a peaceful heart
- a purposeful heart
- an "all-in" heart
- a blessing heart
- a receptive heart
- a generous heart
- an expectant heart
- a persistent heart
- a truth-centered heart

- a watchful heart
- a beautiful heart
- a bold heart
- a determined heart
- a prepared heart
- a glory-filled heart
- a Spirit-led heart
- a tender heart
- a trusting heart
- an understanding heart
- a nurturing heart
- an expressive heart

Thank you, Lord. Amen!

Chapter 24: The Road Ahead

"Life is either a daring adventure, or it is nothing at all." – Helen Keller

What do you see as you look ahead down the road from where you are at this very moment? What do you envision? What has God shown you about the next steps of where He is taking or wants to take you? Do you have a word from Him about where you are right now, about where He is leading you, and about his plans for you? Has He told you anything about what He desires to do in and through you for His kingdom of love, peace, righteousness, and joy?

What things remain in your heart which are still unexpressed and therefore not yet active in the part of the world where you have been called to be His salt and light? What dreams within you remain unexplored, uncharted, undiscovered, and unfulfilled? What promises has God confirmed in your heart that He will do, but you have yet to see Him accomplish them?

How strong and determined is your faith to hold fast to and declare those things for which you have been believing God but are still waiting to see come to pass? How tenacious are you to see the promises of God show up in your life and the lives of those around you—to see Him do mighty and wondrous things so that others can see how good He is and how passionately He loves us?

How willing are you to step out in faith, to boldly and prophetically declare the word of the Lord over your home, family, congregation, place of business, school, community, city, nation, government, and world? How audaciously are you willing to lovingly proclaim what God has already said and done to a skeptical, discouraged, and disillusioned generation? How committed are you to seeing your corner of the world transformed, so that the Lord's Prayer becomes reality? *Thy Kingdom come. Thy will be done, On earth as it is in Heaven.* (Matthew 6:10 NASB)

How adventurously do you look at the opportunities and challenges the Lord is inviting you to embrace? Do you see the possibilities in the impossibilities staring you in the face? Are you willing to launch out into the deep, into the unknown—into whatever God is calling you—wherever He is calling you? Are you willing to abandon everything and just go? Are you? Are you willing to say yes to the greatest adventure you will ever know, of following Him, of holding nothing back, of only going forward, and never looking back?

What is God saying to you right now? What is He really communicating? Are you tuned in? Are you listening? Are you paying attention? Are you ready to respond when He gives you the signal?

God is looking for daring adventurers: men and women of exuberant faith and joy, who will, with complete abandonment, just say *yes* to His call and go forth with Him, knowing that He alone holds their present, past, and future. He is inviting each of us—no matter how young or old; no matter how educated or not; no matter how qualified or not; no matter how experienced or not; no matter how influential or not; no matter how well off or not; no matter how successful or not; no matter how comfortable or not; no matter how settled or not; no matter how respected or not; no matter how prepared or not—to just answer His call and step out fearlessly into the next great adventure He has for us.

The only thing we have to give Him is ourself; it's the only gift we can offer Him. It's the same gift He has already bestowed on those of us who have decided to receive Him and trust Him with our life.

God has offered us all of Himself. It is everything we need and will ever require. It's all found in Him: nothing missing—nothing lacking—everything available—in unlimited abundance. It's more than you could ever imagine, more than you could ever desire, and much more than you could ever dare to ask for. He has it all, and He is offering it—Himself—to us.

Right now I believe God is asking us:

"Will you come and follow Me? Will you dare to trust Me? Will you believe what I have said? Will you do as I have asked? Will you love as I have loved? Will you walk with Me on the road ahead?"

Thou will make known to me the path of life;

In Thy presence is fulness of joy;

In Thy right hand there are pleasures forever. (Psalm 16:11 NASB)

Chapter 25: The Father's Heart For Africa

When God said, ***"Let us make man in Our image, after Our likeness"*** (Genesis 1:26 NASB), He deposited a wonderfully indescribable, glorious part of Himself into every person who would ever be born on this earth. Each of us has received something uniquely precious as a result of being *"made in His image."*

Man's disobeying God and turning away from Him necessitated the greatest rescue mission of all time, when God spared no expense, and sent His only Son, Yeshua/Jesus, to be born and experience life as one of us, to suffer on our behalf, to be resurrected from the dead, to be the only sufficient and ultimate sacrifice for sin and for all of our mistakes and rebellion, and to reclaim all that man had, through deception and disobedience, handed over to the enemy in the Garden of Eden.

Over the millenia, over the centuries, God has had His Eye and His Heart of love and compassion over His chosen covenant people, Abraham and his descendants, and over each people group, each nation, and each continent. He has longed for all of us to open our hearts and to receive the free gift of salvation and restoration that Jesus provided to us at an immeasurably high cost to Himself, so that we could, each one, become the beautiful, glorious reflection of Himself that He imagined, designed, created, and purposed for us to express, for His glory, and to be a blessing to others.

The LORD your God in your midst, A victorious warrior. He will exult over you with joy, He will be quiet in His love, He will rejoice over you with shouts of joy. (Zephaniah 3:17 NASB)

This is the time when I sense the Father saying, *"Africa, I am calling you, each one of you, and all of you, from every family, from every tribe, from every community, village, city, region, and nation, back home to Me, to the place of deep heart intimacy and belonging with Me that I created you for.* ***And everyone who calls on the name of the LORD will be saved;*** *(Joel 2:32 NIV) I am inviting you to return home, to come back to your true identity, to your rightful inheritance, and to your purposed calling. I am asking you to abandon the false gods, idols, and seducing voices and spirits you have followed and worshipped, to turn away from those things which have deceived your minds and stolen your hearts and your destiny, and to embrace Life, found only in the One who came to seek, rescue, save, deliver, redeem, cleanse, and restore all that the enemy of your souls and all who have partnered with him, have stolen.*

I know your pain, your agony, the senseless, barbaric, tragic brutality you have suffered at the hands of those who enslaved and destroyed your bodies, sought to imprison your minds, hearts, and souls, scattered your people across the world, and stole your resources. I alone understand the depths of despair each of you who has lost so much has experienced. I, the Son of man, alone, recognize who you truly are, and are called to be: My beloved sons and daughters! I have something for you, for each one of you to do, for such a time as this, that no one else can accomplish for My Kingdom. **Come to me, all who are weary and heavy laden, and I will give you rest.** (Matthew 11:28 NASB)

I long to receive you unto Myself, so that together, as one, we can begin the unparalleled journey of Faith, Hope, and Love, which abide forevermore, in My Presence. **I have loved you with an everlasting love; Therefore I have drawn you with lovingkindness.** (Jeremiah 31:3 NASB) There is no one else who is and has, all that you need, both now, and forevermore. I am your Source, and your all-encompassing Resource, sufficient for every circumstance and situation.

Now is the time, the appointed moment, in this final season of history, when My Greater Glory is being poured out on all flesh, over all of the earth, to journey home, to the safety, security, and embrace of My strong, loving arms, to ask for and to receive forgiveness, to pardon all those who have transgressed against you, to learn from what is behind and then release it, and to follow Me, through the new door that I am opening for you.

I AM. The King of Glory. The Alpha and Omega. The Almighty One. The Bread of Life. The Good Shepherd. The King of Kings and Lord of Lords. The Lamb of God. The Light of the World. The Lord of All. The Messiah. The Son of Man and Son of the Most High. The Door. The Way. The Truth. The Life. The Word. The Word Made Flesh. The Resurrection and the Life. The Wonderful Counselor, Mighty God, Everlasting Father, Prince of Peace. I AM."

Afterword

On April 6, 2019, the day after I had finished the first round of checking, correcting, and editing the manuscript of this book, I awoke with a short dream about my father still fresh in my memory.

The Dream

I'm sitting at the kitchen table at my brother's house. I think it's a holiday when the immediate family are getting together. I catch sight of my father walking toward the kitchen from the left; I close my eyes and pretend to be asleep. As my father enters the kitchen, I hear him greeted by and talking with another of my brothers about the possibility of his visiting their family during that holiday. That other brother tells him he is sorry, but that won't be a good time for them; I can sense my father's disappointment. Then, I hear the first brother, the one whose house we are in, approaching. He informs my father that dinner is ready and asks if he would like to join them. My father says that he would and enters the dining room. Then, I wake up.

The Dream Interpretation

As I was lying there, wondering about the dream, I sensed the Lord saying to me in my spirit: *"Nowhere in this book have you even mentioned your father or anything about him. Did you not have a father? Have you forgotten My commandment to honor your father and mother?"*

In the dream, I was pretending to be asleep, even though my father was right there in front of me. I would normally have greeted him, given him a hug, and started talking with him, so why didn't I do that?

In the writing of this book, I have only indicated in the dedication that I give thanks for being raised in a family of faith, with no mention of my dad, though he was present during the first thirteen years of my life and made efforts to be my father. Despite his being there during my childhood, our relationship never became a very close one. My father had a very limiting view of roles within marriage. It was also difficult for him to open up and share with our mother and us about his deeper feelings and inner life. As I entered my teen years, my dad started working in another city, spent less and less time at home, and rarely met us. He communicated very little with my mother or with any of us and slowly disappeared from our lives.

My father was an only child and lost both of his parents when he was a baby. His mother died shortly after giving birth to him, and his father passed away about ten months later. My dad never knew his biological parents and was raised by his paternal grandparents. I had never really thought about the effect that must have had on my father and how it had shaped his personality and life. Over the years, I kept in touch with my dad, visited him whenever I returned to Pennsylvania to see family, and also sent him greeting cards and letters several times a year. He often wrote back and sent me cards at Christmas and on my birthday. There was also a period of about two years when we would get together every few weeks, do some kind of fitness activity, and have a meal together. We rarely talked about very personal things—usually just information about the family, his job and mine, current events, or politics. He did periodically encourage me in my faith, however, and several times gave me a book of daily Scripture meditations or a one-year Bible.

After I came to Hungary to teach, I only got to see my dad in the summer when I went home to visit everyone. In the autumn of 1997, my father went home to be with the Lord. My siblings and I were there at his bedside to read Scripture to him and were with him toward the very end of his life. I had long ago forgiven my father for not being there during the teenage years when I needed him the most, and I thought I had made peace with those years of his absence from our lives.

It was only at a three-day, silent, spiritual retreat organized and led by Jesuit brothers and sisters here in Hungary about fifteen years ago, that some deeper issues I had about my father came to the surface. During the first session with my spiritual advisor, I suddenly started sobbing uncontrollably and had no idea why. The tears continued for more than ten minutes, and I could see my advisor was beginning to look concerned. Finally, he asked me if I had any idea what was producing all those tears, and, at that moment, the Lord showed me it was about my father. My spiritual advisor gave me several passages of Scripture to read and pray over that evening and asked me to write down in my journal whatever came to my mind and heart, which I did. During our next session, he asked me to write a letter to my father, followed by a letter to Jesus about my father. At our final meeting, he asked me to write a third letter from my father to me, in response to my letter to him. I had no idea how that was going to work, but as I sat down each time to write and invited the Holy Spirit to guide me, the words and the tears just began to flow. As I wrote each of those letters, the Holy Spirit was doing a deep inner cleansing and healing of those parts of my life and development which had been neglected by my father, and He helped me to fully forgive him and let go of all of the regrets and disappointments I had been carrying deep within me for so many years—things which I was not even consciously aware of.

My mother had the keys to my father's heart; she wanted and tried to help him, but my father couldn't see that everything he needed was right there in front of him. He thought he would find his treasure someplace else, but I don't think he really did. He checked out of the marriage relationship when things were beginning to become more and more difficult, and he missed the amazing marriage God could have enabled him to create with my mother, who would have helped him find a way through those challenges. In a very real sense, my father missed his true destiny and the highest calling of God upon his life. He stopped dreaming and daring to explore and live out all that God had been inviting him to become. I believe that all of us in our family, in different ways, have determined not to make the same mistakes that our father made.

When God instructed us to honor our father and mother, He didn't qualify that by saying that we should only honor them if they live up to our expectations; He just commanded us to honor them. That's why I needed to write this afterword: to simply say that I did have a father who tried, during my childhood years, to love, raise, and support me. During that three-day silent spiritual retreat, I mourned the years of lost father-son relationship that we never experienced, the deeper conversations we never shared, and the untapped potential of all that my father could have become and how that could have influenced a whole generation. I finally made peace with all of that during that retreat, and the Lord helped me to understand, accept, and appreciate my father as he was, with his strengths, limitations, and missed opportunities.

I may be wrong about this, but I have the sense that **the greatest source of undiscovered, unused potential and untapped miracles on this earth is to be found in men's hearts.** It's much easier for a woman to learn to listen to, understand, and live out of her heart than it is for a man to do so. I believe that every man needs a woman of faith who will not only love and honor him, but also teach him how to open his heart. We males simply can't get there on our own; we need a lot of help to understand who we really are, how to truly love, and how to fully step into all that God has called us as men to be. Here's a wonderful quote made by by one of my students at Horváth Mihály Gimnázium many years ago: *"Because if you want to learn to love, you will always remain a student."* [1]

I am thankful to God for the positive things I inherited from my dad: creative and musical gifts, a strong sense of idealism, and the ability to dream the impossible. From my mother, siblings, relatives, and close friends, I have been given wonderful role models and much grace to learn how to step out in faith in practical ways to create the dreams that God has placed in my heart. I'm in the challenging place right now of daring to keep on believing for the seemingly impossible—as nearly everything I felt the Lord was beginning to prepare me for in this new season has seemingly disappeared. Nevertheless, I'm determined to keep pressing onward and upward, taking practical steps, listening to the Holy Spirit, and following His guidance, until I see and experience all that He has shown me is possible. If there is one thing I am certain of, it is that God always has a marvelous plan. His plan is perfect, and we don't need to understand what He is doing; we just have to trust and follow Him. He'll get us to our destination, the one that He has purposed for us, if we'll keep going and refuse to give up hope.

No matter where you are in your life journey, I encourage you to keep listening, waiting, watching, praying, trusting, declaring, standing, giving, receiving, sowing, thanking, sharing, praising, and worshipping. Your breakthrough is much closer than you could ever imagine.

God wants each of us to finish our race—our earthly journey of faith—with great success. It doesn't matter where we start; what matters is how we are going to finish: are we going to finish strong? He is cheering for us, every step of the way. The word *impossible* doesn't even exist in the dictionaries of the Library of Heaven, so I encourage you to delete that word from your earthly dictionary. The Lord is our Coach, and He is training us to win every match, every time. Whenever you find yourself staring at an impossible situation, stand on His unfailing Word, refuse to be moved, pray it through, and declare: *"For nothing will be impossible with God."* (Luke 1:37 NASB)

Notes

Chapter 2 What If

1. Joshua and Rebekah Weigel: *The Butterfly Circus* (August 31, 2009 https://thebutterflycircus.com/

Chapter 5 Seeing Is Believing

1. Dr. Caroline Leaf: *The Perfect You: A Blueprint For Identity* (Forest Hills, MI: Baker Publishing Group, 2017)

Chapter 13 Heart School

1. Socrates: Unsourced quotation

Chapter 16 Thinking Three in the Marriage Relationship

1. K. Gallagher: *Hebrew Numbers 1-10* (June 15, 2015) https://graceintorah.net/2015/06/15/hebrew-numbers-1-10/

Chapter 17 Pure in Heart

1. Winston Churchill: *Reader's Digest, Volume 50* (The Reader's Digest Association, May 1947)

Chapter 19 The Way Back Home

1. Ulrich Shaffer: *Love Reaches Out* (New York, NY: Harper and Row, Publishers, Inc., 1976)

Chapter 24 The Road Ahead

1. Helen Keller: *The Open Door* (Garden City, NJ: Doubleday, 1957)

Afterword

1. Laborczy Éva: *Classwork Writing Task (Szentes, Hungary, 1993)*

Map of Africa

Recommended Reading

Bevere, L. *Lioness Arising*. Colorado Springs, CO: Waterbrook Press, 2010.

Bridges, K. *Invading the Heavens*. Kensington, PA: Whitaker House, 2018.

Chambers, O. *Love: A Holy Command*. Grand Rapids, MI: Discovery House Publishers, 2008.

Drs. Clark, K. and J. *Breaking Soul Ties-Freedom from Toxic Relationships*. Shippensburg, PA: Destiny Image Publishers, Inc., 2019.

Evans, J. *Marriage On The Rock*. Dallas, TX: Marriage Today, 1994, 2009.

Hess, K. *The Warrior Bride*. Jerusalem, Israel: Progressive Vision International, 2017.

Hess, T. *The Watchmen*. Jerusalem, Israel: Progressive Vision International, 2008.

Jacobs, C. *The Voice of God*. Bloomington, MN: Chosen Books, 1995, 2016.

Jakes, T.D. *Making Great Decisions*. New York, NY: Atria Paperback, 2008.

Dr. Leaf, C. *The Perfect You-A Blueprint For Identity*. Forest Hills, MI: Baker Publishing Group, 2017

Dr. Leaf, C. *Switch On Your Brain*. Grand Rapids, MI: Baker Books, 2013.

Meyer, J. *Battlefield of the Mind*. New York, NY: Faith Words Hachette Book Group USA, 1995.

Mills, J. *Moving In Glory Realms*. New Kensington, PA: Whitaker House, 2018.

Munroe, M. *Rediscovering The Kingdom*. Shippensburg, PA: Destiny Image Publishers, Inc., 2004.

Munroe, M. *Understanding the Purpose and Power of Men*. New Kensington, PA: Whitaker House, 2001, 2017.

Munroe, M. *Understanding the Purpose and Power of Women*. New Kensington, PA: Whitaker House, 2001, 2018.

Munroe, M. *The Principles and Power of Vision*. New Kensington, PA: Whitaker House, 2003.

Nouwen, H. *The Inner Voice of Love*. New York, NY: Image Books/Doubleday, 1996.

Dr. Owusu, S. *Dream Again*. Canada: DaySprings Publishing, 2020.

Shook, K. and C. *Love At Last Sight*. Colorado Springs, CO: Waterbook Press, 2010.

Thomas, G. *Sacred Marriage*. Grand Rapids, MI: Zondervan, 2000, 2015.

Virkler M., Virkler Kayembe C. *Hearing God through Your Dreams*. Shippensburg, PA: Destiny Image Publishers, Inc., 2016.

Zadai, K. L. *Praying From The Heavenly Realms*. Shippensburg, PA: Destiny Image Publishers, Inc., 2018

About the Author

Timothy Lehman, a native of Lancaster, Pennsylvania, taught English, French or Spanish at four public high schools in southern Hungary from 1990 to 2019. He most recently taught part-time at Horváth Mihály Gimnázium, Szentes and Táncsics Mihály Gimnázium, Orosháza. In addition to teaching and organizing student theatrical and musical performances, he compiled two books of student writings, co-organized student trips to the U.S. and Israel, and co-ordinated host family stays for Hungarian students in the U.S. Prior to completing his M.A. in Teaching from the School for International Training, Timothy worked as a YMCA Professional Director in Illinois and Connecticut. He preached monthly at the Szentes Baptist Congregation from 2016 to 2020 and has represented Hungary four times as a delegate to the Jerusalem House of Prayer for All Nations Convocation. He has a passion for helping young people discover their gifting, calling, and purposed identity to become sons and daughters of the Most High God.

Printed in the United States
by Baker & Taylor Publisher Services